Dale Carnegie was
motivational speal
pioneered instructio
self-motivation and personality development which helped millions. He was the author of *How to Win Friends and Influence People* and *How to Stop Worrying and Start Living*, both of which are popular bestsellers even today. He also wrote *Lincoln the Unknown* among many other books. Dale Carnegie died in 1955.

YOUR PERSONAL GUIDE TO BIG SUCCESS

DALE CARNEGIE

SPEAKING
TIGER

SPEAKING TIGER PUBLISHING PVT. LTD
4381/4, Ansari Road, Daryaganj
New Delhi 110002

ISBN: 978-93-88070-74-4
eISBN: 978-93-88070-73-7

10 9 8 7 6 5 4 3 2 1

Typeset in Adobe Garamond Pro by SÜRYA, New Delhi
Printed at Gopsons Papers Ltd.

CONTENTS

A NOTE TO THE READER

Easily among the best known, and most inspirational, thinkers, writers and teachers of the twentieth century, Dale Carnegie was born into poverty in a farmer's family in Missouri and made a success out of himself through hard work and sheer determination. He was, at different times, a salesman and an actor before he became a motivational speaker who taught students, businessmen, and executives in the corporate world. He also developed self-improvement courses that were meant for everyone, from students and executives to housewives, which inspired people to be the best that they could be. In his lifetime Dale Carnegie wrote a number of hugely popular books which taught by examples—from his own life, the lives of successful corporate and political leaders of the time, and the people who attended his classes—what we must do if we are to be good communicators, likeable people with a large network of loyal friends, and successful, happy and contented individuals in our professional and personal spaces.

Drawing from across Dale Carnegie's writings, and specially put together for you by the publishers, this handy volume distils the essential, timeless principles imparted by Dale Carnegie which have inspired millions over the decades to positively shape their careers and lives. Each easy, direct principle is illustrated by stories and anecdotes. Also included at the end are a selection of quotes on success and achievement by Dale Carnegie himself and the thinkers and achievers he most admired.

Whether you are a young person with big life decisions to make, a professional newly entering your career, or a seasoned hand with many years of experience, you will find something for yourself in this special compilation. Apply these lessons and principles, and gain from them.

TAKE THE TIME TO FIND A CAREER THAT YOU WOULD MOST ENJOY AND EXCEL AT

If you are under eighteen, you will probably soon be called upon to make the two most important decisions of your life—decisions that will profoundly alter all the days of your years: decisions that may have far-reaching effects upon your happiness, your income, your health; decisions that may make or break you. What are these two tremendous decisions?

First: How are you going to make a living? Are you going to be a farmer, a mail carrier, a chemist, a forest ranger, a stenographer, a horse dealer, a college professor, or are you going to run a hamburger stand?

Second: Whom are you going to select to be the father or mother of your children?

Both of those great decisions are frequently gambles. "Every boy," says Harry Emerson Fosdick in his book, *The Power to See It Through*, "every boy is a gambler when he chooses a vocation. He must stake his life on it."

How can you reduce the gamble in selecting a vocation? Read on; we will tell you as best we can. First, try, if possible, to find work that you enjoy. I once asked David M. Goodrich, Chairman of the Board, B. F. Goodrich Company—tyre manufacturers—what he considered the first requisite of success in business, and he replied: "Having a good time at your work. If you enjoy what you are doing," he said, "you may work long hours, but it won't seem like work at all. It will seem like play."

Edison was a good example of that. Edison—the unschooled newsboy who grew up to transform the industrial life of America—Edison, the man who often ate and slept in his laboratory and toiled there for eighteen hours a day. But it wasn't toil to him. "I never did a day's work in my life," he exclaimed. "It was all fun!"

No wonder he succeeded!

I once heard Charles Schwab say much the same thing. He said: "A man can succeed at almost anything for which he has unlimited enthusiasm."

But how can you have enthusiasm for a job when you haven't the foggiest idea of what you want to do? "The greatest tragedy I know of," said Mrs. Edna Kerr, who once hired thousands of employees for the Dupont Company, and is now assistant director of industrial relations for the American Home Products Company—"The greatest tragedy I know of," she told me, "is that so many young people never discover what they really want to do. I think no one else is so much to be pitied as the person who gets nothing at all out of his work but his pay." Mrs. Kerr reports that even college graduates come to her and say: "I have a B.A. degree from Dartmouth [or an M.A. from Cornell]. Have you some kind of work I can do for your firm?" They don't know themselves what they are able to do, or even what they would like to do. Is it any wonder that so many men and women who start out in life with competent minds and rosy dreams end up at forty in utter frustration and even with a nervous breakdown? In fact, finding the right occupation is important even for your health. When Dr. Raymond Pearl, of Johns Hopkins, made a study, together with some insurance companies, to discover the factors that make for a long life, he placed "the right occupation" high on the list. He might have said, with Thomas Carlyle: "Blessed is the man who has found his work. Let him ask no other blessedness."

I recently spent an evening with Paul W. Boynton, employment supervisor for the Socony-Vacuum Oil Company. During the last twenty years he has interviewed more than seventy-five thousand people looking for jobs, and he has written a book entitled *6 Ways to Get a Job*. I asked him: "What is the greatest mistake young people make today in looking for work?" "They don't know what they want to do," he said. "It is perfectly appalling to realise that a man will give more thought to buying a suit of clothes that will wear out in a few years than he will give to choosing the career on which his whole future depends—on which his whole future happiness and peace of mind are based!"

And so what? What can you do about it? You can take advantage of a new profession called vocational guidance. It may help you—or harm you—depending on the ability and character of the counselor you consult. This new profession isn't even within gunshot of perfection yet. It hasn't even reached the Model T stage. But it has a great future. How can you make use of this science? By finding out where, in your community, you can get vocational tests and vocational advice.

Such advice can only take the form of

suggestions. You have to make the decisions. Remember that these counselors are far from infallible. They don't always agree with one another. They sometimes make ridiculous mistakes. For example, a vocational-guidance counselor advised one of my students to become a writer solely because she had a large vocabulary. How absurd! It isn't as simple as that. Good writing is the kind that transfers your thoughts and emotions to the reader—and to do that, you don't need a large vocabulary, but you do need ideas, experience, convictions, examples and excitement. The vocational counselor who advised this girl with a large vocabulary to become an author succeeded in doing only one thing: he turned an erstwhile happy stenographer into a frustrated, would-be novelist.

The point I am trying to make is that vocational-guidance experts, even as you and I, are not infallible. Perhaps you had better consult several of them—and then interpret their findings in the sunlight of common sense…

Many of our worries, regrets, and frustrations are spawned by work we despise. Ask your father about it—or your neighbour or your boss. No less an intellectual giant than John Stuart Mill declared that industrial misfits are "among the heaviest losses of society". Yes, and among the unhappiest people on this earth are those same "industrial misfits" who hate their daily work!

Do you know the kind of man who "cracked up" in the Army? The man who was misplaced! I'm not talking about battle casualties, but about the men who cracked up in ordinary service. Dr. William Menninger, one of our greatest living psychiatrists, was in charge of the Army's neuro-psychiatric division during the war, and he says: "We learned much in the Army as to the importance of selection and of placement, of putting the right man in the right job. A conviction of the importance of the job at hand was extremely important. Where a man had no interest, where he felt he was misplaced, where he thought he was not appreciated, where he believed his talents were being misused, invariably we found a potential if not an actual psychiatric casualty."

Yes—and for the same reasons, a man may "crack up" in industry. If he despises his business, he can crack it up, too.

Take, for example, the case of Phil Johnson. Phil Johnson's father owned a laundry, so he gave his son a job, hoping the boy would work into the business. But Phil hated the laundry, so he dawdled, loafed, did what he had to do and not a lick more. Some days he was "absent". His father was so hurt to think he had a shiftless, ambitionless son that he was actually ashamed before his employees.

One day Phil Johnson told his father he wanted to be a mechanic—work in a machine shop. What? Go back to overalls? The old man was shocked. But Phil had his way. He worked in greasy dungarees. He did much harder work than was required at the laundry. He worked longer hours, and he whistled at his job! He took up engineering, learned about engines, puttered with machines—and when Philip Johnson died, in 1944, he was president of the Boeing Aircraft Company, and was making the Flying Fortresses that helped to win the war! If he had stuck with the laundry, what would have happened to him and the laundry—especially after his father's death? My guess is he would have ruined the business—cracked it up and run it into the ground.

Even at the risk of starting family fights, I would like to say to young people: Don't feel compelled to enter a business or trade just because your family wants you to do it! Don't enter a career unless you want to do it! However, consider carefully the advice of your parents. They have probably lived twice as long as you have. They have gained the kind of wisdom that comes only from much experience and the passing of many years. But, in the last analysis, you are the one who has to make the final decision. You are the one who is going to be either happy or miserable at your work.

Now, having said this, let me give you the following suggestions—some of them warnings—about choosing your work:

1. Read and study the following five suggestions about selecting a vocational-guidance counselor. These suggestions are right from the horse's mouth. They were made by one of America's leading vocational-guidance experts, Professor Harry Dexter Kitson of Columbia University.
    a. "Don't go to anyone who tells you that he has a magic system that will indicate your 'vocational aptitude'. In this group are phrenologists, astrologers, 'character analysts', handwriting experts. Their 'systems' do not work."

b. "Don't go to anyone who tells you that he can give you a test that will indicate what occupation you should choose. Such a person violates the principle that a vocational counselor must take into account the physical, social, and economic conditions surrounding the counselee; and he should render his service in the light of the occupational opportunities open to the counselee."

c. "Seek a vocational counselor who has an adequate library of information about occupations and uses it in the counseling process."

d. "A thorough vocational-guidance service generally requires more than one interview."

e. "Never accept vocational guidance by mail."

2. Keep out of business and professions that are already jam-packed and overflowing! There are many thousands of different ways of making a living. But do young people know this? Not unless they hire a swami to gaze

into a crystal ball. The result? In one school, two-thirds of the boys confined their choices to five occupations—five out of twenty thousand—and four-fifths of the girls did the same. Small wonder that a few business and professions are overcrowded—small wonder that insecurity, worry, and "anxiety neuroses" are rampant at times among the white-collar fraternity. Beware of trying to elbow your way into such overcrowded fields as law, journalism, radio, motion pictures, and the "glamour occupations".

3. Stay out of activities where the chances are only one out of ten of your being able to make a living. As an example, take selling life insurance. Each year countless thousands of men—frequently unemployed men—start out trying to sell life insurance without bothering to find out in advance what is likely to happen to them! Here is approximately what does happen, according to Franklin L. Bettger, Real Estate Trust Building, Philadelphia. For twenty years Mr. Bettger was one of the outstandingly successful insurance salesmen in America. He declares

that ninety per cent of the men who start selling life insurance get so heartsick and discouraged that they give it up within a year. Out of the ten who remain, one man will sell ninety per cent of the insurance sold by the group of ten; and the other nine will sell only ten per cent. To put it another way: if you start selling life insurance, the chances are nine to one that you will fail and quit within twelve months, and the chances are only one in a hundred that you will make ten thousand a year out of it. Even if you remain at it, the chances are only one out of ten that you will be able to do anything more than barely scratch out a living.

4. Spend weeks—even months, if necessary—finding out all you can about an occupation before deciding to devote your life to it! How? By interviewing men and women who have already spent ten, twenty, or forty years in that occupation.

These interviews, with the veterans of their respective fields, may have a profound effect on your future. I know that from my own experience. When

I was in my early twenties, I sought the vocational advice of two older men. As I look back now, I can see that those two interviews were turning points in my career. In fact, it would be difficult for me even to imagine what my life would have been like had I not had those two interviews.

How can you get these vocational-guidance interviews? To illustrate, let's suppose that you are thinking about studying to be an architect. Before you make your decision, you ought to spend weeks interviewing the architects in your city and in adjoining cities. You can get their names and addresses out of a classified telephone directory. You can call at their offices either with or without an appointment. If you wish to make an appointment, write them something like this:

Won't you please do me a little favour? I want your advice. I am eighteen years old, and I am thinking about studying to be an architect. Before I make up my mind, I would like to ask your advice.

If you are too busy to see me at your office, I would be most grateful if you would grant me the privilege of seeing you for half an hour at your home.

Here is a list of questions I would like to ask you:

a. If you had your life to live over, would you become an architect again?
b. After you have sized me up, I want to ask you whether you think I have what it takes to succeed as an architect.
c. Is the profession of architecture overcrowded?
d. If I studied architecture for four years, would it be difficult for me to get a job? What kind of job would I have to take at first?
e. If I had average ability, how much could I hope to earn during the first five years?
f. What are the advantages and disadvantages of being an architect?
g. If I were your son, would you advise me to become an architect?

If you are timid, and hesitate to face a "big shot" alone, here are two suggestions that will help.

First, get a lad of your own age to go with you. The two of you will bolster up one another's confidence. If you haven't someone of your own age to go with you, ask your father to go with you.

Second, remember that by asking his advice you are paying this man a compliment. He may feel flattered by your request. Remember that adults like to give advice to young men and women. The architect will probably enjoy the interview.

If you hesitate to write letters asking for an appointment, then go to a man's office without an appointment and tell him you would be most grateful if he would give you a bit of advice.

Suppose you call on five architects and they are all too busy to see you (which isn't likely), call on five more. Some of them will see you and give you priceless advice—advice that may save you years of lost time and heartbreak.

Remember that you are making one of the two most vital and far-reaching decisions of your life. So, take time to get the facts before you act. If you don't, you may spend half a lifetime regretting it.

If you can afford to do so, offer to pay a man for a half-hour of his time and advice.

5. Get over the mistaken belief that you are fitted for only a single occupation! Every normal person can succeed at a number of occupations, and every normal person would probably fail in many occupations. Take myself, for example: if I had studied and prepared myself for the following occupations,

I believe I would have had a good chance of achieving some small measure of success—and also of enjoying my work. I refer to such occupations as farming, fruit-growing, scientific agriculture, medicine, selling, advertising, editing a country newspaper, teaching, and forestry. On the other hand, I am sure I would have been unhappy, and a failure, at bookkeeping, accounting, engineering, operating a hotel or a factory, architecture, all mechanical trades, and hundreds of other activities.

WIN PEOPLE OVER TO YOUR POINT OF VIEW AND INSPIRE ACTION

There is only one way under high heaven to get anybody to do anything. Did you ever stop to think of that? Yes, just one way. And that is by making the other person want to do it. Remember, there is no other way.

One of the first people in American business to be paid a salary of over a million dollars a year (when there was no income tax and a person earning fifty dollars a week was considered well off) was Charles Schwab. He had been picked by Andrew Carnegie to become the first president of the newly formed United States Steel Company in 1921, when Schwab was only thirty-eight years old. (Schwab later left U.S. Steel to take over the then-troubled Bethlehem Steel Company, and he rebuilt it into one of the most profitable companies in America.)

Why did Andrew Carnegie pay a million dollars a year, or more than three thousand dollars a day, to Charles Schwab? Why? Because Schwab was a genius? No. Because he knew more about the manufacture of steel than other people? Nonsense. Charles Schwab told me himself that he had many men working for him who knew more about the manufacture of steel than he did.

Schwab says that he was paid this salary largely because of his ability to deal with people. I asked him how he did it. Here is his secret set down in his own words—words that ought to be cast in eternal bronze and hung in every home and school, every shop and office in the land—words that children ought to memorize instead of wasting their time memorizing the conjugation of Latin verbs or the amount of the annual rainfall in Brazil—words that will all but transform your life and mine if we will only live them:

"I consider my ability to arouse enthusiasm among my people," said Schwab, "the greatest asset I possess, and the way to develop the best that is in a person is by appreciation and encouragement.

"There is nothing else that so kills the ambitions of a person as criticisms from superiors. I never criticize anyone. I believe in giving a person incentive to work. So I am anxious to praise but loath to find fault. If I like anything, I am hearty in my approbation and lavish in my praise."

That is what Schwab did. But what do average people do? The exact opposite. If they don't like a thing, they bawl out their subordinates; if they do like it, they say nothing. As the old couplet says: "Once I did bad and that I heard ever/Twice I did good, but that I heard never."

"In my wide association in life, meeting with many and great people in various parts of the world," Schwab declared, "I have yet to find the person, however great or exalted his station, who did not do better work and put forth greater effort under a spirit of approval than he would ever do under a spirit of criticism."

~

Many years ago a boy of ten was working in a factory in Naples, He longed to be a singer, but his first teacher discouraged him. "You can't sing," he said. "You haven't any voice at all. It sounds like the wind in the shutters."

But his mother, a poor peasant woman, put her arms about him and praised him and told him she knew he could sing, she could already see an improvement, and she went barefoot in order to save money to pay for his music lessons.

That peasant mother's praise and encouragement changed that boy's life. His name was Enrico Caruso, and he became the greatest and most famous opera singer of his age.

~

In the early nineteenth century, a young man in London aspired to be a writer. But everything seemed to be against him. He had never been able to attend school more than four years. His father had been flung in jail because he couldn't pay his debts, and this young man often knew the pangs of hunger. Finally, he got a job pasting labels on bottles of blacking in a rat-infested warehouse, and he slept at night in a dismal attic room with two other boys—guttersnipes from the slums of London. He had so little confidence in his ability to write that he sneaked out and mailed his first manuscript in the dead of night so nobody would laugh at him. Story after story was refused. Finally the great day came when one was accepted. True, he wasn't paid a shilling for it, but one editor had praised him. One editor had given him recognition. He was so thrilled that he wandered aimlessly around the streets with tears rolling down his cheeks.

The praise, the recognition, that he received through getting one story in print, changed his whole life, for if it hadn't been for that encouragement, he might have spent his entire life working in rat-infested factories.

You may have heard of that boy. His name was Charles Dickens.

~

Another boy in London made his living as a clerk in a dry-goods store. He had to get up at five o'clock, sweep out the store, and slave for fourteen hours a day. It was sheer drudgery and he despised it. After two years, he could stand it no longer, so he got up one morning and, without waiting for breakfast, tramped fifteen miles to talk to his mother, who was working as a housekeeper.

He was frantic. He pleaded with her. He wept. He swore he would kill himself if he had to remain in the shop any longer. Then he wrote a long, pathetic letter to his old schoolmaster, declaring that he was heartbroken, that he no longer wanted to live. His old schoolmaster gave him a little praise and assured him that he really was very intelligent and fitted for finer things and offered him a job as a teacher.

That praise changed the future of that boy and made a lasting impression on the history of English literature. For that boy went on to write innumerable best-selling books and made over a million dollars with his pen.

You've probably heard of him. His name: H.G. Wells.

~

We nourish the bodies of our children and friends and employees, but how seldom do we nourish their self-esteem? We provide them with roast beef and potatoes to build energy, but we neglect to give them kind words of appreciation that would sing in their memories for years like the music of the morning stars.

Paul Harvey, in one of his radio broadcasts, "The Rest of the Story," told how showing sincere appreciation can change a person's life. He reported that years ago a teacher in Detroit asked Stevie Morris to help her find a mouse that was lost in the classroom. You see, she appreciated the fact that nature had given Stevie something no one else in the room had. Nature had given Stevie a remarkable pair of ears to compensate for his blind eyes.

But this was really the first time Stevie had been shown appreciation for those talented ears. Now, years later, he says that this act of appreciation was the beginning of a new life. You see, from that time on he developed his gift of hearing and went on to become, under the stage name of Stevie Wonder, one of the great pop singers and and songwriters of the seventies.

~

Some readers are saying right now as they read these lines: "Oh, phooey! *Flattery! Bear oil!* I've tried that stuff. It doesn't work—not with intelligent people."

Of course flattery seldom works with discerning people. It is shallow, selfish and insincere. It ought to fail and it usually does...

The difference between appreciation and flattery? That is simple. One is sincere and the other insincere. One comes from the heart out; the other from the teeth out. One is unselfish; the other selfish. One is universally admired; the other universally condemned...

One of the most neglected virtues of our daily existence is appreciation. Somehow, we neglect to praise our son or daughter when he or she brings home a good report card, and we fail to encourage our children when they first succeed in baking a cake or building a birdhouse. Nothing pleases children more than this kind of parental interest and approval...

Every minister, lecturer and public speaker knows the discouragement of pouring himself or herself out to an audience and not receiving a single ripple of appreciative comment. What applies to professionals applies doubly to workers in offices, shops and factories and our families and friends. In our interpersonal relations we should never forget that all our associates are human beings and hunger for appreciation. It is the legal tender that all souls enjoy.

Try leaving a friendly trail of little sparks of gratitude on your daily trips. You will be surprised how they will set small flames of friendship that will be rose beacons on your next visit.

~

Hurting people not only does not change them, it is never called for. There is an old saying that I have cut out and pasted on my mirror where I cannot help but see it every day: 'I shall pass this way but once; any good, therefore, that I can do or any kindness that I can show to any human being, let me do it now. Let me not defer nor neglect it, for I shall not pass this way again.'

Emerson said: "Every man I meet is my superior in some way, In that, I learn of him."

If that was true of Emerson, isn't it likely to be a thousand times more true of you and me? Let's cease thinking of our accomplishments, our wants. Let's try to figure out the other person's good points. Then forget flattery. Give honest, sincere appreciation. Be "hearty in your approbation and lavish in your praise," and people will cherish your words and treasure them and repeat them over a lifetime—repeat them years after you have forgotten them.

BE GENUINELY INTERESTED IN PEOPLE TO BUILD STRONG PERSONAL AND WORK RELATIONSHIPS

To be interesting, be interested. Ask questions that other persons will enjoy answering. Encourage them to talk about themselves and their accomplishments. Remember that the people you are talking to are a hundred times more interested in themselves and their wants and problems than they are in you and your problems.

I was waiting in line to register a letter in the post office at Thirty-third Street and Eighth Avenue in New York. I noticed that the clerk appeared to be bored with the job—weighing envelopes, handing out stamps, making change, issuing receipts—the same monotonous grind year after year. So I said to myself: "I am going to try to make that clerk like me. Obviously, to make him like me, I must say something nice, not about myself, but about him. So I asked myself, 'What is there about him that I can honestly admire?'

"That is sometimes a hard question to answer, especially with strangers; but, in this case, it happened to be easy. I instantly saw something I admired no end. So while he was weighing my envelope, I remarked with enthusiasm: "I certainly wish I had your head of hair."

He looked up, half-startled, his face beaming with smiles. "Well, it isn't as good as it used to be," he said modestly. I assured him that although it might have lost some of its pristine glory, nevertheless it was still magnificent.

He was immensely pleased. We carried on a pleasant little conversation and the last thing he said to me was: "Many people have admired my hair."

I'll bet that person went out to lunch that day walking on air. I'll bet he went home that night and told his wife about it. I'll bet he looked in the mirror and said: "It is a beautiful head of hair."

I told this story once in public and a man asked me afterwards: "'What did you want to get out of him?"

What was I trying to get out of him! What was I trying to get out of him!

If we are so contemptibly selfish that we can't radiate a little happiness and pass on a bit of honest appreciation without trying to get something out of the other person in return—if our souls are no bigger than sour crab apples, we shall meet with the failure we so richly deserve.

Oh yes, I did want something out of that chap. I wanted something priceless. And I got it. I got the feeling that I had done something for him without his being able to do anything whatever in return for me. That is a feeling that flows and sings in your memory long after the incident is past.

~

George Eastman, of Kodak fame, invented the transparent film that made motion pictures possible, amassed a fortune of a hundred million dollars, and made himself one of the most famous businessmen on earth. Yet in spite of all these tremendous accomplishments, he craved little recognitions even as you and I.

To illustrate: When Eastman was building the Eastman School of Music and also Kilbourn Hall in Rochester, James Adamson, then president of the Superior Seating Company of New York, wanted to get the order to supply the theater chairs for these buildings. Phoning the architect,

Mr. Adamson made an appointment to see Mr. Eastman in Rochester.

When Adamson arrived, the architect said: "I know you want to get this order, but I can tell you right now that you won't stand a ghost of a show if you take more than five minutes of George Eastman's time. He is a strict disciplinarian. He is very busy. So tell your story quickly and get out."

Adamson was prepared to do just that.

When he was ushered into the room he saw Mr. Eastman bending over a pile of papers at his desk. Presently, Mr. Eastman looked up, removed his glasses, and walked toward the architect and Mr. Adamson, saying: "Good morning, gentlemen, what can I do for you?"

The architect introduced them, and then Mr. Adamson said: "While we've been waiting for you, Mr. Eastman, I've been admiring your office. I wouldn't mind working in a room like this myself. I'm in the interior-woodworking business, and I never saw a more beautiful office in all my life."

George Eastman replied: "You remind me of something I had almost forgotten. It is beautiful, isn't it? I enjoyed it a great deal when it was first built. But I come down here now with a lot of other things on my mind and sometimes don't even see the room for weeks at a time."

Adamson walked over and rubbed his hand across a panel. "This is English oak, isn't it? A little different texture from Italian oak."

"Yes," Eastman replied. "Imported English oak. It was selected for me by a friend who specializes in fine woods."

Then Eastman showed him about the room, commenting on the proportions, the coloring, the hand carving and other effects he had helped to plan and execute. While drifting about the room, admiring the wood-work, they paused before a window, and George Eastman, in his modest, soft-spoken way, pointed out some of the institutions through which he was trying to help humanity: the University of Rochester, the General Hospital, the Homeopathic Hospital, the Friendly Home, the Children's Hospital.

Mr. Adamson congratulated him warmly on the idealistic way he was using his wealth to alleviate the sufferings of humanity. Presently, George Eastman unlocked a glass case and pulled out the first camera he had ever owned—an invention he had bought from an Englishman.

Adamson questioned him at length about his early struggles to get started in business, and Mr. Eastman spoke with real feeling about the poverty of his childhood, telling how his widowed mother had kept a boardinghouse while he clerked in an insurance office. The terror of poverty haunted him day and night, and he resolved to make enough money so that his mother wouldn't have to work, Mr. Adamson drew him out with further questions and listened, absorbed, while he related the story of his experiments with dry photographic plates. He told how he had worked in an office all day, and sometimes experimented all night, taking only brief naps while the chemicals were working, sometimes working and sleeping in his clothes for seventy-two hours at a stretch.

James Adamson had been ushered into Eastman's office at ten-fifteen and had been warned that he must not take more than five minutes; but an hour had passed, then two hours passed. And they were still talking. Finally, George Eastman turned to Adamson and said, "The last time I was in Japan I bought some chairs, brought them home, and put them in my sun porch. But the sun peeled the paint, so I went downtown the other day and bought some paint and painted the chairs myself. Would you like to see what sort of a job I can do painting chairs? All right. Come up to my home and have lunch with me and I'll show you."

After lunch, Mr. Eastman showed Adamson the chairs he had brought from Japan. They weren't worth more than a few dollars, but George Eastman, now a multimillionaire, was proud of them because he himself had painted them.

The order for the seats amounted to $90,000. Who do you suppose got the order—James Adamson or one of his competitors?

From the time of this story until Mr. Eastman's death, he and James Adamson were close friends.

~

Charles R. Walters, of one of the large banks in New York City, was assigned to prepare a confidential report on a certain corporation. He knew of only one person who possessed the facts he needed so urgently. As Mr. Walters was ushered into the president's office, a young woman stuck her head through a door and told the president that she didn't have any stamps for him that day.

"I am collecting stamps for my twelve-year-old son," the president explained to Mr. Walters.

Mr. Walters stated his mission and began asking questions. The president was vague, general, nebulous. He didn't want to talk, and apparently nothing could persuade him to talk. The interview was brief and barren.

"Frankly, I didn't know what to do," Mr. Walters said as he related the story to the class. "Then I remembered what his secretary had said to him—stamps, twelve-year-old son… And I also recalled that the foreign department of our bank collected stamps—stamps taken from letters pouring in from every continent washed by the seven seas.

"The next afternoon I called on this man and sent in word that I had some stamps for his boy. Was I ushered in with enthusiasm? Yes sir, he couldn't have shaken my hand with more enthusiasm if he had been running for Congress. He radiated smiles and good will. 'My George will love this one,' he kept saying as he fondled the stamps. 'And look at this! This is a treasure.'

"We spent half an hour talking stamps and looking at a picture of his boy, and he then devoted more than an hour of his time to giving me every bit of information I wanted—without my even suggesting that he do it. He told me all he knew, and then called in his subordinates and questioned them. He telephoned some of his associates. He loaded me down with facts, figures, reports and correspondence. In the parlance of newspaper reporters, I had a scoop."

~

Here is another illustration:

C.M. Knaphle, Jr., of Philadelphia had tried for years to sell fuel to a large chain-store organization. But the chain-store company continued to purchase its fuel from an out-of-town dealer and haul it right past the door of Knaphle's office. Mr, Knaphle made a speech one night before one of my classes, pouring out his hot wrath upon chain stores, branding them as a curse to the nation.

And still he wondered why he couldn't sell them. I suggested that he try different tactics. To put it briefly, this is what happened. We staged a debate between members of the course on whether the spread of the chain store is doing the country more harm than good. Knaphle, at my suggestion, took the negative side; he agreed to defend the chain stores, and then went straight to an executive of the chain-store organization that he despised and said: "I am not here to try to sell fuel. I have come to ask you to do me a favor." He then told about his debate and said, "I have come to you for help because I can't think of anyone else who would be more capable of giving me the facts I want. I'm anxious to win this debate, and I'll deeply appreciate whatever help you can give me."

Here is the rest of the story in Mr. Knaphle's own words:

I had asked this man for precisely one minute of his time. It was with that understanding that he consented to see me. After I had stated my case, he motioned me to a chair and talked to me for exactly one hour and forty-seven minutes. He called in another executive who had written a book on chain stores. He wrote to the National Chain Store Association and secured for me a copy of a debate on the subject. He feels that the chain store is rendering a real service to humanity. He is proud of what he is doing for hundreds of communities. His eyes fairly glowed as he talked, and I must confess that he opened my eyes to things I had never even dreamed of. He changed my whole mental attitude. As I was leaving, he walked with me to the door, put his arm around my shoulder, wished me well in my debate, and asked me to stop in and see him again and let him know how I made out. The last words he said to me were: "Please see me again later in the spring. I should like to place an order with you for fuel."

To me that was almost a miracle. Here he was offering to buy fuel without my even suggesting it. I had made more headway in two hours by becoming genuinely interested in him and his problems than I could have made in ten years trying to get him interested in me and my product.

You didn't discover a new truth, Mr. Knaphle, for a long time ago, a hundred years before Christ was born a famous old Roman poet, Publilius Syrus, remarked: "We are interested in others when they are interested in us."

A show of interest, as with every other principle of human relations, must be sincere. It must pay off not only for the person showing the interest, but for the person receiving the attention. It is a two-way street—both parties benefit.

Alfred Adler, the famous Viennese psychologist, wrote a book entitled *What Life Should Mean to*

You. In that book he says: "It is the individual who is not interested in his fellow men who has the greatest difficulties in life and provides the greatest injury to others. It is from among such individuals that all human failures spring."

You may read scores of erudite tomes on psychology without coming across a statement more significant for you and for me.

~

Years ago, a poor Dutch immigrant boy washed the windows of a bakery shop after school to help support his family. His people were so poor that in addition he used to go out in the street with a basket every day and collect stray bits of coal that had fallen in the gutter where the coal wagons had delivered fuel. That boy, Edward Bok, never got more than six years of schooling in his life; yet eventually he made himself one of the most successful magazine editors in the history of American journalism. How did he do it? That is a long story, but how he got his start can be told briefly.

He left school when he was thirteen and became an office boy for Western Union, but he didn't for one moment give up the idea of an education. Instead, he started to educate himself. He saved his carfares and went without lunch until he had enough money to buy an encyclopedia of American biography—and then he did an unheard-of thing. He read the lives of famous people and wrote them asking for additional information about their childhoods. He was a good listener. He asked famous people to tell him more about themselves. He wrote General James A. Garfield, who was then running for President, and asked if it was true that he was once a tow boy on a canal, and Garfield replied. He wrote General Grant asking about a certain battle, and Grant drew a map for him and invited this fourteen-year-old boy to dinner and spent the evening talking to him.

Soon our Western Union messenger boy was corresponding with many of the most famous people in the nation: Ralph Waldo Emerson, Oliver Wendell Holmes, Longfellow, Mrs. Abraham Lincoln, Louisa May Alcott, General Sherman and Jefferson Davis. Not only did he correspond with these distinguished people, but as soon as he got a vacation, he visited many of them as a welcome guest in their homes. This experience imbued him with a confidence that was invaluable. These men and women fired him with a vision and ambition that shaped his life.

~

An angry customer stormed into the office of Julian F. Detmer, founder of the Detmer Woolen Company, which later became the world's largest distributor of woolens to the tailoring trade. "This man owed us a small sum of money," Mr. Detmer explained to me. "The customer denied it, but we knew he was wrong. So our credit department had insisted that he pay. After getting a number of letters from our credit department, he packed his grip, made a trip to Chicago, and hurried into my office to inform me not only that he was not going to pay that bill, but that he was never going to buy another dollar's worth of goods from the Detmer Woolen Company.

"I listened patiently to all he had to say. I was tempted to interrupt, but I realized that would be bad policy, So I let him talk himself out. When he finally simmered down and got in a receptive mood, I said quietly: 'I want to thank you for coming to Chicago to tell me about this. You have done me a great favor, for if our credit department has annoyed you, it may annoy other good customers, and that would be just too bad. Believe me, I am far more eager to hear this than you are to tell it.'

"That was the last thing in the world he expected me to say. I think he was a trifle disappointed, because he had come to Chicago to tell me a thing or two, but here I was thanking him instead of scrapping with him. I assured him we would wipe the charge off the books and forget it, because he was a very careful man with only one account to look after, while our clerks had to look after thousands. Therefore, he was less likely to be wrong than we were.

"I told him that I understood exactly how he felt and that, if I were in his shoes, I should undoubtedly feel precisely as he did. Since he wasn't going to buy from us anymore, I recommended some other woolen houses.

"In the past, we had usually lunched together when he came to Chicago, so I invited him to have lunch with me this day. He accepted reluctantly, but when we came back to the office he placed a larger order than ever before. He returned home in a softened mood and, wanting to be just as fair with us as we had been with him, looked over his bills, found one that had been mislaid, and sent us a check with his apologies.

"Later, when his wife presented him with a baby boy, he gave his son the middle name of Detmer, and he remained a friend and customer of the house until his death twenty-two years afterwards."

~

What was the reason for Andrew Carnegie's success? He was called the Steel King; yet he himself knew little about the manufacture of steel. He had hundreds of people working for him who knew far more about steel than he did. But he knew how to handle people, and that is what made him rich. Early in life, he showed a flair for organization, a genius for leadership. By the time he was ten, he too had discovered the astounding importance people place on their own name. And he used that discovery to win cooperation.

To illustrate: When he was a boy back in Scotland, he got hold of a rabbit, a mother rabbit. Presto! He soon had a whole nest of little rabbits—and nothing to feed them. But he had a brilliant idea. He told the boys and girls in the neighborhood that if they would go out and pull enough clover and dandelions to feed the rabbits, he would name the bunnies in their honor. The plan worked like magic, and Carnegie never forgot it.

Years later, he made millions by using the same psychology in business. For example, he wanted to sell steel rails to the Pennsylvania Railroad. J. Edgar Thomson was the president of the Pennsylvania Railroad then.

So Andrew Carnegie built a huge steel mill in Pittsburgh and called it the "Edgar Thomson Steel Works."

Here is a riddle. See if you can guess it. When the Pennsylvania Railroad needed steel rails, where do you suppose J. Edgar Thomson bought them? From Sears, Roebuck? No. No. You're wrong. Guess again.

When Carnegie and George Pullman were battling each other for supremacy in the railroad sleeping-car business, the Steel King again remembered the lesson of the rabbits.

The Central Transportation Company, which Andrew Carnegie controlled, was fighting with the company that Pullman owned. Both were struggling to get the sleeping-car business of the

Union Pacific Railroad, bucking each other, slashing prices, and destroying all chance of profit. Both Carnegie and Pullman had gone to New York to see the board of directors of the Union Pacific.

Meeting one evening in the St. Nicholas Hotel, Carnegie said: "Good evening, Mr. Pullman, aren't we making a couple of fools of ourselves?"

"What do you mean.?" Pullman demanded.

Then Carnegie expressed what he had on his mind—a merger of their two interests. He pictured in glowing terms the mutual advantages of working with, instead of against, each other. Pullman listened attentively, but he was not wholly convinced. Finally he asked, "What would you call the new company?" and Carnegie replied promptly: "Why, the Pullman Palace Car Company, of course."

Pullman's face brightened. "Come into my room," he said. "Let's talk it over." That talk made industrial history.

~

There is one all-important law of human conduct. If we obey that law, we shall almost never get into trouble. In fact, that law, if obeyed, will bring us countless friends and constant happiness. But the very instant we break the law, we shall get into endless trouble. The law is this: Always make the other person feel important...

Philosophers have been speculating on the rules of human relationships for thousands of years, and out of all that speculation, there has evolved only one important precept. It is not new. It is as old as history. Zoroaster taught it to his followers in Persia twenty-five hundred years ago. Confucius preached it in China twenty-four centuries ago. Lao-tse, the founder of Taoism, taught it to his disciples in the Valley of the Han. Buddha preached it on the bank of the Holy Ganges five hundred years before Christ. The sacred books of Hinduism taught it a thousand years before that. Jesus taught it among the stony hills of Judea nineteen centuries ago. Jesus summed it up in one thought—probably the most important rule in the world: "Do unto others as you would have others do unto you."

You want the approval of those with whom you come in contact. You want recognition of your true worth. You want a feeling that you are important in your little world. You don't want to listen to cheap, insincere flattery, but you do crave sincere appreciation. You want your friends and associates to be, as Charles Schwab put it, "hearty in their approbation and lavish in their praise." All of us want that.

So let's obey the Golden Rule, and give unto others what we would have others give unto us, How? When? Where? The answer is: All the time, everywhere.

LEARN HOW TO CRITICISE WITHOUT OFFENDING; INSTEAD, INSPIRE CHANGE

Criticism is futile because it puts a person on the defensive and usually makes him strive to justify himself. Criticism is dangerous, because it wounds a person's precious pride, hurts his sense of importance, and arouses resentment.

The Wark Company had contracted to build and complete a large office building in Philadelphia by a certain specified date. Everything was going along well; the building was almost finished, when suddenly the sub-contractor making the ornamental bronze work to go on the exterior of this building declared that he couldn't make delivery on schedule. What! An entire building held up! Heavy penalties! Distressing losses! All because of one man! Long-distance telephone calls. Arguments! Heated conversations! All in vain. Then Mr. Gaw was sent to New York to beard the bronze lion in his den.

"Do you know you are the only person in Brooklyn with your name?" Mr Gaw asked the president of the subcontracting firm shortly after they were introduced.

The president was surprised. "No, I didn't know that."

"Well," said Mr. Gaw, "when I got off the train this morning, I looked in the telephone book to get your address, and you're the only person in the Brooklyn phone book with your name."

"I never knew that," the subcontractor said. He checked the phone book with interest. "Well, it's an unusual name," he said proudly. "My family came from Holland and settled in New York almost two hundred years ago." He continued to talk about his family and his ancestors for several minutes. When he finished that, Mr. Gaw complimented him on how large a plant he had and compared it favorably with a number of similar plants he had visited. "It is one of the cleanest and neatest bronze factories I ever saw," said Gaw.

"I've spent a lifetime building up this business," the subcontractor said, "and I am rather proud of it. Would you like to take a look around the factory?"

During this tour of inspection, Mr. Gaw complimented the other man on his system of fabrication and told him how and why it seemed superior to those of some of his competitors. Gaw commented on some unusual machines, and the subcontractor announced that he himself had invented those machines. He spent considerable time showing Gaw how they operated and the superior work they turned out. He insisted on taking his visitor to lunch. So far, mind you, not a word had been said about the real purpose of Gaw's visit.

After lunch, the subcontractor said, "Now, to get down to business. Naturally, I know why you're here. I didn't expect that our meeting would be so enjoyable. You can go back to Philadelphia with my promise that your material will be fabricated and shipped, even if other orders have to be delayed."

Mr. Gaw got everything that he wanted without even asking for it. The material arrived on time, and the building was completed on the day the completion contract specified. Would this have happened had Mr. Gaw used the hammer-and-dynamite method generally employed on such occasions?

~

Ms. Mazzone, a marketing specialist for a food packer, was given her first major assignment—the test-marketing of a new product. She told the class: "When the results of the test came in, I was devastated. I had made a serious error in my planning, and the entire test had to be done all over again. To make this worse, I had no time to discuss it with my boss before the meeting in which I was to make my report on the project.

"When I was called on to give the report, I was shaking with fright. I had all I could do to keep from breaking down, but I resolved I would not cry and have all those men make remarks about women not being able to handle a management job because they are too emotional. I made my report briefly and stated that due to an error I would repeat the study before the next meeting. I sat down, expecting my boss to blow up.

"Instead, he thanked me for my work and remarked that it was not unusual for a person to make an error on a new project and that he had confidence that the repeat survey would be accurate and meaningful to the company. He assured me, in front of all my colleagues, that he had faith in me and I knew I had done my best, and that my lack of experience, not my lack of ability, was the reason for the failure.

I left that meeting with my head in the air and with the determination that I would never let that boss of mine down again."

Even if we are right and the other person is definitely wrong, we only destroy ego by causing someone to lose face. The legendary French aviation pioneer and author Antoine de Saint-Exupéry wrote: "I have no right to say or do anything that diminishes a man in his own eyes. What matters is not what I think of him, but what he thinks of himself. Hurting a man in his dignity is a crime."

~

My niece, Josephine Carnegie, had come to New York to be my secretary. She was nineteen, had graduated from high school three years previously, and her business experience was a trifle more than zero. She became one of the most proficient secretaries west of Suez, but in the beginning, she was—well, susceptible to improvement. One day when I started to criticize her, I said to myself: "Just a minute, Dale Carnegie; just a minute. You are twice as old as Josephine. You have had ten thousand times as much business experience. How can you possibly expect her to have your viewpoint, your judgment, your initiative—mediocre though they may be? And just a minute, Dale, what were you doing at nineteen? Remember the asinine mistakes and blunders you made? Remember the time you did this…and that…?"

After thinking the matter over, honestly and impartially, I concluded that Josephine's batting average at nineteen was better than mine had been—and that, I'm sorry to confess, isn't paying Josephine much of a compliment.

So after that, when I wanted to call Josephine's attention to a mistake, I used to begin by saying, "You have made a mistake, Josephine, but the Lord knows, it's no worse than many I have made. You were not born with judgment. That comes only with experience, and you are better than I was at your age. I have been guilty of so many stupid, silly things myself, I have very little inclination to criticize you or anyone. But don't you think it would have been wiser if you had done so and so?"

It isn't nearly so difficult to listen to a recital of your faults if the person criticizing begins by humbly admitting that he, too, is far from impeccable.

~

E.G. Dillistone, an engineer in Brandon, Manitoba, Canada, was having problems with his new secretary. Letters he dictated were coming to his desk for signature with two or three spelling mistakes per page. Mr. Dillistone reported how he handled this: "Like many engineers, I have not been noted for my excellent English or spelling. For years I have kept a little black thumb-index book for words I had trouble spelling. When it became apparent that merely pointing out the errors was not going to cause my secretary to do more proofreading and dictionary work, I resolved to take another approach. When the next letter came to my attention that had errors in it, I sat down with the typist and said: "'Somehow this word doesn't look right. It's one of the words I always have had trouble with. That's the reason I started this spelling book of mine. [I opened the book to the appropriate page.] Yes, here it is. I'm very conscious of my spelling now because people do judge us by our letters and misspellings make us look less professional.

"I don't know whether she copied my system or not, but since that conversation, her frequency of spelling errors has been significantly reduced."

Admitting one's own mistakes—even when one hasn't corrected them—can help convince somebody to change his behavior.

~

As Lincoln lay dying, Secretary of War Stanton said, "There lies the most perfect ruler of men that the world has ever seen."

What was the secret of Lincoln's success in dealing with people? I studied the life of Abraham Lincoln for ten years and devoted all of three years to writing and rewriting a book entitled *Lincoln the Unknown*. I believe I have made as detailed and exhaustive a study of Lincoln's personality and home life as it is possible for any being to make. I made a special study of Lincoln's method of dealing with people. Did he indulge in criticism? Oh, yes. As a young man in the Pigeon Creek Valley of Indiana, he not only criticized but he wrote letters and poems ridiculing people and dropped these letters on the country roads where they were sure to be found. One of these letters aroused resentments that burned for a lifetime.

Even after Lincoln had become a practicing lawyer in Springfield, Illinois, he attacked his opponents openly in letters published in the newspapers. But he did this just once too often.

In the autumn of 1842 he ridiculed a vain, pugnacious politician by the name of James Shields. Lincoln lamned him through an anonymous letter published in *Springfield Journal.* The town roared with laughter. Shields, sensitive and proud, boiled with indignation. He found out who wrote the letter, leaped on his horse, started after Lincoln, and challenged him to fight a duel.

Lincoln didn't want to fight. He was opposed to dueling, but he couldn't get out of it and save his honor. He was given the choice of weapons. Since he had very long arms, he chose cavalry broadswords and took lessons in sword-fighting from a West Point graduate; and, on the appointed day, he and Shields met on a sandbar in the Mississippi River, prepared to fight to the death; but, at the last minute, their seconds interrupted and stopped the duel.

That was the most lurid personal incident in

Lincoln's life. It taught him an invaluable lesson in the art of dealing with people. Never again did he write an insulting letter. Never again did he ridicule anyone. And from that time on, he almost never criticized anybody for anything.

~

The Battle of Gettysburg was fought during the first three days of July 1863. During the night of July 4, Lee began to retreat southward while storm clouds deluged the country with rain. When Lee reached the Potomac with his defeated army, he found a swollen, impassable river in front of him, and a victorious Union Army behind him. Lee was in a trap. He couldn't escape. Lincoln saw that. Here was a golden, heaven-sent opportunity, the opportunity to capture Lee's army and end the war immediately. So, with a surge of high hope, Lincoln ordered Meade not to call a council of war but to attack Lee immediately. Lincoln telegraphed his orders and then sent a special messenger to Meade demanding immediate action.

And what did General Meade do? He did the very opposite of what he was told to do. He called a council of war in direct violation of Lincoln's orders.

He hesitated. He procrastinated. He telegraphed all manner of excuses. He refused point-blank to attack Lee. Finally the waters receded and Lee escaped over the Potomac with his forces.

Lincoln was furious, "What does this mean?" Lincoln cried to his son Robert. "Great God! What does this mean? We had them within our grasp, and had only to stretch forth our hands and they were ours; yet nothing that I could say or do could make the army move. Under the circumstances, almost any general could have defeated Lee. If I had gone up there, I could have whipped him myself."

In bitter disappointment, Lincoln sat down and wrote Meade this letter. And remember, at this period of his life Lincoln was extremely conservative and restrained in his phraseology. So this letter coming from Lincoln in 1863 was tantamount to the severest rebuke.

> My dear General,
>
> I do not believe you appreciate the magnitude of the misfortune involved in Lee's escape. He was within our easy grasp, and to have closed upon him would, in connection with our other late successes, have ended

> the war. As it is, the war will be prolonged indefinitely. If you could not safely attack Lee last Monday, how can you possibly do so south of the river, when you can take with you very few, no more than two-thirds of the force you then had in hand?
>
> It would be unreasonable to expect and I do not expect that you can now effect much. Your golden opportunity is gone, and I am distressed immeasurably because of it.

What do you suppose Meade did when he read the letter? Meade never saw that letter. Lincoln never mailed it. It was found among his papers after his death. My guess is—and this is only a guess—that after writing that letter, Lincoln looked out of the window and said to himself, "Just a minute. Maybe I ought not to be so hasty. It is easy enough for me to sit here in the quiet of the White House and order Meade to attack; but if I had been up at Gettysburg, and if I had seen as much blood as Meade has seen during the last week, and if my ears had been pierced with the screams and shrieks of the wounded and dying, maybe I wouldn't be so anxious to attack either. If I had Meade's timid temperament, perhaps I would have done just what he had done. Anyhow, it is water under the bridge now. If I send this letter, it will relieve my feelings, but it will make Meade try to justify himself. It will make him condemn me. It will arouse hard feelings, impair all his further usefulness as a commander, and perhaps force him to resign from the army."

So, as I have already said, Lincoln put the letter aside, for he had learned by bitter experience that sharp criticisms and rebukes almost invariably end in futility.

~

Any fool can criticize, condemn and complain—and most fools do. But it takes character and self-control to be understanding and forgiving.

REMEMBER, ARGUMENTS ARE THE EASIEST WAY TO MAKE ADVERSARIES

Jesus said: "Agree with thine adversary quickly." And 2,200 years before Christ was born, King Akhtoi of Egypt gave his son some shrewd advice—advice that is sorely needed today. "Be diplomatic," counseled the King. "It will help you gain your point." In other words, don't argue with your customer or your spouse or your adversary. Don't tell them they are wrong, don't get them stirred up. Use a little diplomacy.

Over three hundred years ago Galileo said: 'You cannot teach a man anything; you can only help him to find it within himself.' Lord Chesterfield said to his son: 'Be wiser than other people if you can; but do not tell them so.' Socrates said repeatedly to his followers in Athens: 'One thing only I know, and that is that I know nothing.'

Well, I can't hope to be any smarter than Socrates, so I have quit telling people they are wrong. And I find that it pays. If a person makes a statement that you think is wrong—yes, even that you know is wrong—isn't it better to begin by saying: "Well, now, look, I thought otherwise, but I may be wrong. I frequently am. And if I am wrong, I want to be put right. Let's examine the facts."

There's magic, positive magic, in such phrases as: "I may be wrong. I frequently am. Let's examine the facts."

~

Shortly after the close of World War I, I learned an invaluable lesson one night in London. I was manager at the time for Sir Ross Smith. During the war, Sir Ross had been the Australian ace out in Palestine; and shortly after peace was declared, he astonished the world by flying halfway around it in thirty days. No such feat had ever been attempted before. It created a tremendous sensation. The Australian government awarded him fifty thousand dollars; the King of England knighted him; and, for a while, he was the most talked-about man under the Union Jack. I was attending a banquet one night given in Sir Ross's honor; and during the dinner, the man sitting next to me told a humorous story which hinged on the quotation "There's a divinity that shapes our ends, rough-hew them how we will."

The raconteur mentioned that the quotation was from the Bible. He was wrong. I knew that, I knew it positively. There couldn't be the slightest doubt about it.

And so, to get a feeling of importance and display my superiority, I appointed myself as an unsolicited and unwelcome committee of one to correct him. He stuck to his guns. What? From Shakespeare? Impossible! Absurd! That quotation was from the Bible. And he knew it.

The storyteller was sitting on my right; and Frank Gammond, an old friend of mine, was seated at my left. Mr. Gammond had devoted years to the study of Shakespeare, so the storyteller and I agreed to submit the question to Mr. Gammond. Mr. Gammond listened, kicked me under the table, and then said: "Dale, you are wrong. The gentleman is right. It is from the Bible."

On our way home that night, I said to Mr. Gammond: "Frank, you knew that quotation was from Shakespeare,"

"Yes, of course," he replied, "*Hamlet*, Act Five, Scene Two. But we were guests at a festive occasion, my dear Dale. Why prove to a man he is wrong? Is that going to make him like you? Why not let him save his face? He didn't ask for your opinion. He didn't want it. Why argue with him? Always avoid the acute angle."

The man who said that taught me a lesson I'll never forget. I not only had made the storyteller uncomfortable, but had put my friend in an embarrassing situation. How much better it would have been had I not become argumentative.

It was a sorely needed lesson because I had been an inveterate arguer. During my youth, I had argued with my brother about everything under the Milky Way. When I went to college, I studied logic and argumentation and went in for debating contests. Talk about being from Missouri, I was born there. I had to be shown.

Later, I taught debating and argumentation in New York; and once, I am ashamed to admit, I planned to write a book on the subject. Since then, I have listened to, engaged in, and watched the effect of thousands of arguments. As a result of all this, I have come to the conclusion that there is only one way under high heaven to get the best of an argument—and that is to avoid it...

Nine times out of ten, an argument ends with each of the contestants more firmly convinced than ever that he is absolutely right. You can't win an argument. You can't because if you lose it, you lose it; and if you win it, you lose it. Why?

Well, suppose you triumph over the other man and shoot his argument full of holes and prove that he is non compos mentis. Then what? You will feel fine. But what about him? You have made him feel inferior. You have hurt his pride. He will resent your triumph. And:

A man convinced against his will
Is of the same opinion still.

~

Katherine A. Allred of Kings Mountain, North Carolina, is an industrial engineering supervisor for a yarn-processing plant. She told one of our classes how she handled a sensitive problem before and after taking our training:

"Part of my responsibility," she reported, "deals with setting up and maintaining incentive systems and standards for our operators so they can make more money by producing more yarn.

The system we were using had worked fine when we had only two or three different types of yarn, but recently we had expanded our inventory and capabilities to enable us to run more than twelve different varieties. The present system was no longer adequate to pay the operators fairly for the work being performed and give them an incentive to increase production. I had worked up a new system which would enable us to pay the operator by the class of yarn she was running at any one particular time. With my new system in hand, I entered the meeting determined to prove to the management that my system was the right approach. I told them in detail how they were wrong and showed where they were being unfair and how I had all the answers they needed. To say the least, I failed miserably! I had become so busy defending my position on the new system that I had left them no opening to graciously admit their problems on the old one. The issue was dead.

"After several sessions of this course, I realized all too well where I had made my mistakes. I called another meeting and this time I asked where they felt their problems were. We discussed each point, and I asked them their opinions on which was the best way to proceed.

With a few low-keyed suggestions, at proper intervals, I let them develop my system themselves. At the end of the meeting when I actually presented my system, they enthusiastically accepted it.

"I am convinced now that nothing good is accomplished and a lot of damage can be done if you tell a person straight out that he or she is wrong. You only succeed in stripping that person of self-dignity and making yourself an unwelcome part of any discussion."

~

Let's take another example—and remember these cases I am citing are typical of the experiences of thousands of other people.

R.V. Crowley was a salesman for a lumber company in New York. Crowley admitted that he had been telling hard-boiled lumber inspectors for years that they were wrong. And he had won the arguments too. But it hadn't done any good. "For these lumber inspectors," said Mr. Crowley, "are like baseball umpires. Once they make a decision, they never change it."

Mr. Crowley saw that his firm was losing thousands of dollars through the arguments he won. So while taking my course, he resolved to change tactics and abandon arguments. With what results? Here is the story as he told it to the fellow members of his class:

"One morning the phone rang in my office. A hot and bothered person at the other end proceeded to inform me that a car of lumber we had shipped into his plant was entirely unsatisfactory. His firm had stopped unloading and requested that we make immediate arrangements to remove the stock from their yard. After about one-fourth of the car had been unloaded, their lumber inspector reported that the lumber was running 55 percent below grade. Under the circumstances, they refused to accept it.

"I immediately started for his plant and on the way turned over in my mind the best way to handle the situation. Ordinarily, under such circumstances, I should have quoted grading rules and tried, as a result of my own experience and knowledge as a lumber inspector, to convince the other inspector that the lumber was actually up to grade, and that he was misinterpreting the rules in his inspection. However, I thought I would apply the principles learned in this training.

"When I arrived at the plant, I found the

purchasing agent and the lumber inspector in a wicked humor, both set for an argument and a fight. We walked out to the car that was being unloaded, and I requested that they continue to unload so that I could see how things were going. I asked the inspector to go right ahead and lay out the rejects, as he had been doing, and to put the good pieces in another pile.

"After watching him for a while it began to dawn on me that his inspection actually was much too strict and that he was misinterpreting the rules. This particular lumber was white pine, and I knew the inspector was thoroughly schooled in hard woods but not a competent, experienced inspector on white pine. White pine happened to be my own strong suit, but did I offer any objection to the way he was grading the lumber? None whatever. I kept on watching and gradually began to ask questions as to why certain pieces were not satisfactory. I didn't for one instant insinuate that the inspector was wrong. I emphasized that my only reason for asking was in order that we could give his firm exactly what they wanted in future shipments.

"By asking questions in a very friendly, cooperative spirit, and insisting continually that they were right in laying out boards not satisfactory to their purpose, I got him warmed up, and the strained relations between us began to thaw and melt away. An occasional carefully put remark on my part gave birth to the idea in his mind that possibly some of these rejected pieces were actually within the grade that they had bought, and that their requirements demanded a more expensive grade. I was very careful, however, not to let him think I was making an issue of this point.

"Gradually his whole attitude changed. He finally admitted to me that he was not experienced on white pine and began to ask me questions about each piece as it came out of the car, I would explain why such a piece came within the grade specified, but kept on insisting that we did not want him to take it if it was unsuitable for their purpose. He finally got to the point where he felt guilty every time he put a piece in the rejected pile. And at last he saw that the mistake was on their part for not having specified as good a grade as they needed.

"The ultimate outcome was that he went through the entire carload again after I left, accepted the whole lot, and we received a check in full.

"In that one instance alone, a little tact, and the determination to refrain from telling the other man he was wrong, saved my company a substantial amount of cash, and it would be hard to place a money value on the goodwill that was saved."

~

Within a minute's walk of my house there was a wild stretch of virgin timber, where the blackberry thickets foamed white in the springtime, where the squirrels nested and reared their young, and the horseweeds grew as tall as a horse's head. This unspoiled woodland was called Forest Park—and it was a forest, probably not much different in appearance from what it was when Columbus discovered America. I frequently walked in this park with Rex, my little Boston bulldog. He was a friendly, harmless little hound; and since we rarely met anyone in the park, I took Rex along without a leash or a muzzle.

One day we encountered a mounted policeman in the park, a policeman itching to show his authority.

"'What do you mean by letting that dog run loose in the park without a muzzle and leash?" he reprimanded me. "Don't you know it's against the law?"

"Yes, I know it is," I replied softy, "but I didn't think he would do any harm out here."

"You didn't think! You didn't think! The law doesn't give a tinker's damn about what you think. That dog might kill a squirrel or bite a child. Now, I'm going to let you off this time; but if I catch this dog out here again without a muzzle and a leash, you'll have to tell it to the judge."

I meekly promised to obey.

And I did obey—for a few times. But Rex didn't like the muzzle, and neither did I; so we decided to take a chance. Everything was lovely for a while, and then we struck a snag. Rex and I raced over the brow of a hill one afternoon and there, suddenly—to my dismay—I saw the majesty of the law, astride a bay horse. Rex was out in front, heading straight for the officer.

I was in for it. I knew it. So I didn't wait until the policeman started talking. I beat him to it. I said: "Officer, you've caught me red-handed. I'm guilty. I have no alibis, no excuses. You warned me last week that if I brought the dog out here again without a muzzle you would fine me."

"Well, now," the policeman responded in a soft tone. "I know it's a temptation to let a little dog like that have a run out here when nobody is around."

"Sure it's a temptation," I replied, "but it is against the law."

"Well, a little dog like that isn't going to harm anybody," the policeman remonstrated.

"No, but he may kill squirrels," I said.

"Well now, I think you are taking this a bit too seriously," he told me. "I'll tell you what you do. You just let him run over the hill there where I can't see him—and we'll forget all about it."

That policeman, being human, wanted a feeling of importance; so when I began to condemn myself, the only way he could nourish his self-esteem was to take the magnanimous attitude of showing mercy.

But suppose I had tried to defend myself—well, did you ever argue with a policeman?

But instead of breaking lances with him, I admitted that he was absolutely right and I was absolutely wrong; I admitted it quickly, openly, and with enthusiasm. The affair terminated graciously in my taking his side and his taking my side.

If you're wrong, admit it.

~

You can tell people they are wrong by a look or an intonation or a gesture just as eloquently as you can in words—and if you tell them they are wrong, do you make them want to agree with you? Never! For you have struck a direct blow at their intelligence, judgment, pride and self-respect. That will make them want to strike back. But it will never make them want to change their minds. You may then hurl at them all the logic of a Plato or an Immanuel Kant, but you will not alter their opinions, for you have hurt their feelings.

Never begin by announcing: "I am going to prove so-and-so to you." That's bad. That's tantamount to saying: "I'm smarter than you are, I'm going to tell you a thing or two and make you change your mind."

That is a challenge. It arouses opposition and makes the listener want to battle with you before you even start.

It is difficult, under even the most benign conditions, to change people's minds. So why make it harder? Why handicap yourself? If you are going to prove anything, don't let anybody know it. Do it so subtly, so adroitly, that no one will feel that you are doing it. This was expressed succinctly by Alexander Pope:

Men must be taught as if you taught them not
And things unknown proposed as things forgot.

SPEAK WITH CONFIDENCE AND CLARITY FOR PROFESSIONAL SUCCESS

The gaining of self-confidence and courage, and the ability to think calmly and clearly while talking to a group is not one-tenth as difficult as most people imagine... Anyone can develop his own latent capacity if he has sufficient desire to do so.

Years ago, a gentleman called Mr. D.W. Ghent, joined my public speaking course in Philadelphia. Shortly after the opening session, he invited me to lunch with him in the Manufacturers' Club. He was a man of middle age and had always led an active life; was head of his own manufacturing establishment, a leader in church work and civic activities. While we were having lunch that day, he leaned across the table and said: "I have been asked many times to talk before various gatherings, but I have never been able to do so. I get so fussed, my mind becomes an utter blank: so I have sidestepped it all my life. But I am chairman now of a board of college trustees. I must preside at their meetings. I simply have to do some talking. Do you think it will be possible for me to learn to speak at this late date in my life?"

"Do I think, Mr. Ghent?" I replied. "It is not a question of my thinking. I *know* you can, and I know you will if you will only practice and follow the directions and instructions."

He wanted to believe that, but it seemed too rosy, too optimistic. "I am afraid you are just being kind," he answered, "that you are merely trying to encourage me."

After he had completed his training, we lost touch with each other for a while. Later, we met and lunched together again at the Manufacturers' Club. We sat in the same corner and occupied the same table that we had had on the first occasion. Reminding him of our former conversation, I asked him if I had been too sanguine then. He took a little red-backed notebook out of his pocket and showed me a list of talks and dates for which he was booked. "And the ability to make these," he confessed, "the pleasure I get in doing it, the additional service I can render to the community—these are among the most gratifying things in my life."

An important disarmament conference had

been held in Washington shortly before that. When it was known that the British Prime Minister was planning to attend it, the Baptists of Philadelphia cabled, inviting him to speak at a great mass meeting to be held in their city. And Mr. Ghent informed me that he himself had been chosen, from among all the Baptists of that city, to introduce England's premier to the audience.

And this was the man who had sat at that same table less than three years before and solemnly asked me if I thought he would ever be able to talk in public!

Was the rapidity with which he forged ahead in his speaking ability unusual? Not at all. There have been hundreds of similar cases. For example—to quote one more specific instance years ago—a Brooklyn physician, whom we will call Dr. Curtis, spent the winter in Florida near the training grounds of the Giants. Being an enthusiastic baseball fan, he often went to see them practice. In time, he became quite friendly with the team and was invited to attend a banquet given in their honor.

After the coffee and nuts were served, several prominent guests were called upon to "say a few words." Suddenly, with the abruptness and unexpectedness of an explosion, he heard the toastmaster remark: "We have a physician with us tonight, and I am going to ask Dr. Curtis to talk on Baseball Players' Health."

Was he prepared? Of course. He had had the best preparation in the world: he had been studying hygiene and practicing medicine for almost a third of a century. He could have sat in his chair and talked about this subject all night to the man seated on his right or left. But to get up and say the same things to even a small audience—that was another matter. That was a paralyzing matter. His heart doubled its pace and skipped beats at the very contemplation of it. He had never made a public speech in his life, and every thought that he had had now took wings.

What was he to do? The audience was applauding. Everyone was looking at him. He shook his head. But that served only to heighten the applause, to increase the demand. The cries of "Dr. Curtis! Speech! Speech!" grew louder and more insistent. He was in positive misery. He knew that if he got up he would fail, that he would be unable to utter half a dozen sentences. So he arose, and, without saying a word, turnedhis back on his friends and walked silently out of the room, a deeply embarrassed and humiliated man.

Small wonder that one of the first things he did after getting back to Brooklyn was to enroll in my course in Public Speaking. He didn't propose to be put to the blush and be stricken dumb a second time.

He was the kind of student that delights an instructor: he was in dead earnest. He wanted to be able to talk, and there was no halfheartedness about his desire. He prepared his talks thoroughly, he practiced them with a will, and he never missed a single session of the course.

He did precisely what such a student always does: he progressed at a rate that surprised him, that surpassed his fondest hopes. After the first few sessions his nervousness subsided, his confidence mounted higher and higher. In two months he had become the star speaker of the group. He was soon accepting invitations to speak elsewhere; he now loved the feel and exhilaration of it, the distinction and the additional friends it brought him.

A member of the New York City Republican Campaign Committee, hearing one of his public addresses, invited Dr. Curtis to stump the city for his party. How surprised that politician would have been had he realized that only a year before, the speaker had gotten up and left a public banquet hall in shame and confusion because he was tongue-tied with audience-fear!

The gaining of self-confidence and courage, and the ability to think calmly and clearly while talking to a group is not one-tenth as difficult as most people imagine. It is not a gift bestowed by Providence on only a few rarely endowed individuals. It is like the ability to play golf. Anyone can develop his own latent capacity if he has sufficient desire to do so.

Is there the faintest shadow of a reason why you should not be able to think as well in a perpendicular position before an audience as you can when sitting down? Surely, you know there is not. In fact, you ought to think better when facing a group. Their presence ought to stir you and lift you. A great many speakers will tell you that the presence of an audience is a stimulus, an inspiration, that drives their brains to function more clearly, more keenly. At such times, thoughts, facts, ideas that they did not know they possessed, "drift smoking by," as Henry Ward Beecher said; and they have but to reach out and lay their hands hot upon them. That ought to be your experience. It probably will be if you practice and persevere.

Of this much, however, you may be absolutely sure: training and practice will wear away your audience-fright and give you self-confidence and an abiding courage. Do not imagine that your case is unusually difficult. Even those who afterward became the most eloquent representatives of their generation were, at the outset of their careers, afflicted by this blinding fear and self-consciousness.

William Jennings Bryan, battle-marked veteran that he was, admitted that in his first attempts, his knees fairly smote together.

Mark Twain, the first time he stood up to lecture, felt as if his mouth were filled with cotton and his pulse were speeding for some prize cup.

Grant took Vicksburg and led to victory one of the greatest armies the world had ever seen up to that time; yet, when he attempted to speak in public, he admitted he had something very like locomotor ataxia.

After watching the careers and aiding somewhat in the development of so many speakers, the author is always glad when a student has, at the outset, a certain amount of flutter and nervous agitation.

There is a certain responsibility in making a talk, even if it is to only two dozen men or women in a business meeting—a certain strain, a certain shock, a certain excitement. The speaker ought to be keyed up like a thoroughbred straining at the bit. The immortal Cicero said, two thousand years ago, that all public speaking of real merit was characterized by nervousness.

Speakers often experience this same feeling even when they are talking over the radio. "Microphone fright," it is called. When Charlie Chaplin went on the air, he had his speech all written out. Surely he was used to audiences. He toured this country back in 1912 with a vaudeville sketch entitled "A Night in a Music Hall." Before that he was on the legitimate stage in England. Yet, when he went into the padded room and faced the microphone, he had a feeling in the stomach not unlike the sensation one gets when he crosses the Atlantic during a stormy February.

~

In order to get the most out of your efforts to become a good speaker in public, and to get it with rapidity and dispatch, four things are essential:

First: Start with a strong and persistent desire

This is of far more importance than you probably realize. If an instructor could look into your mind and heart now and ascertain the depth of your desires, he could foretell, almost with certainty, the swiftness of the progress you will make.

If your desire is pale and flabby, your achievements will also take on that hue and consistency. But, if you go after your subject with persistence, and with the energy of a bulldog after a cat, nothing underneath the Milky Way will defeat you.

Therefore, arouse your enthusiasm for this self-study. Enumerate its benefits. Think of what additional self-confidence and the ability to talk more convincingly in public will mean to you. Think of what it may mean and what it ought to mean, in dollars and cents. Think of what it may mean to you socially; of the friends it will bring, of the increase of your personal influence, of the leadership it will give you. And it will give you leadership more rapidly than almost any other activity you can think of or imagine.

"There is no other accomplishment," stated Chauncey M. Depew, "which any man can have that will so quickly make for him a career and secure recognition as the ability to speak acceptably,"

Philip D. Armour, after he had amassed millions, said: I would rather have been a great speaker than a great capitalist."

It is an attainment that almost every person of education longs for. After Andrew Carnegie's death there was found, among his papers, a plan for his life drawn up when he was thirty-three years of age. He then felt that in two more years he could so arrange his business as to have an annual income of fifty thousand; so he proposed to retire at thirty-five, go to Oxford and get a thorough education, and "pay special attention to speaking in public".

Think of the glow of satisfaction and pleasure that will accrue from the exercise of this new power. The author has traveled around over no small part of the world; and has had many and varied experiences; but for downright and lasting inward satisfaction, he knows of few things that will compare to standing before an audience and making men think your thoughts after you. It will give you a sense of strength, a feeling of power. It will appeal to your pride of personal accomplishment. It will set you off from and raise you above your fellow men. There is magic in it and a never-to-be-forgotten thrill.

"Two minutes before I begin," a speaker confessed, "I would rather be whipped than start; but two minutes before I finish, I would rather be shot than stop."

In every effort, some men grow faint-hearted and fall by the wayside; so you should keep thinking of what this skill will mean to you until your desire is white hot. You should start this program with an enthusiasm that will carry you through triumphant to the end. Set aside one certain night of the week for the reading of these chapters. In short, make it as easy as possible to go ahead. Make it as difficult as possible to retreat.

When Julius Caesar sailed over the channel from Gaul and landed with his legions on what is now England, what did he do to insure the success of his arms? A very clever thing: he halted his soldiers on the chalk cliffs of Dover, and, looking down over the waves two hundred feet below, they saw red tongues of fire consume every ship in which they had crossed. In the enemy's country, with the last link with the Continent gone, the last means of retreating burned, there was but one thing left for them to do: to advance, to conquer. That is precisely what they did.

Such was the spirit of the immortal Caesar. Why not make it yours, too, in this war to exterminate any foolish fear of audiences?

Second: Know thoroughly what you are going to talk about

Unless a person has thought out and planned his talk and knows what he is going to say, he can't feel very comfortable when he faces his auditors. He is like the blind leading the blind. Under such circumstances, your speaker ought to be self-conscious, ought to feel repentant, ought to be ashamed of his negligence.

"I was elected to the Legislature in the fall of 1881," Teddy Roosevelt wrote in his *Autobiography*, "and found myself the youngest man in that body. Like all young men and inexperienced members, I had considerable difficulty in teaching myself to speak. I profited much by the advice of a hard-headed old countryman—who was unconsciously paraphrasing the Duke of Wellington, who was himself doubtless paraphrasing somebody else. The advice ran: 'Don't speak until you are sure you have something to say, and know just what it is; then say it, and sit down.'

This "hard-headed old countryman" ought to have told Roosevelt of another aid in overcoming nervousness. He ought to have added: "It will help you to throw off embarrassment if you can find something to do before an audience—if you can exhibit something, write a word on the blackboard, or point out a spot on the map, or move a table, or throw open a window, or shift some books and papers—any physical action with a purpose behind it may help you to feel more at home."

True, it is not always easy to find an excuse for doing such things; but there is the suggestion. Use it if you can; but use it the first few times only. A baby does not cling to chairs after it once learns to walk.

Third: Act confident

One of the most famous psychologists that America has produced, Professor William James, wrote as follows:

> Action seems to follow feeling, but really action and feeling go together; and by regulating the action, which is under the more direct control

> of the will, we can indirectly regulate the feeling, which is not.
>
> Thus the sovereign voluntary path to cheerfulness, if our spontaneous cheerfulness be lost, is to sit up cheerfully and to act and speak as if cheerfulness were already there. If such conduct does not make you feel cheerful, nothing else on that occasion can.
>
> So, to feel brave, act as if we were brave, use all of our will to that end, and a courage fit will very likely replace the fit of fear.

Apply Professor James' advice. To develop courage when you are facing an audience, act as if you already had it. Of course, unless you are prepared, all the acting in the world will avail but little. But granted that you know what you are going to talk about, step out briskly and take a deep breath. In fact, breathe deeply for thirty seconds before you ever face your audience. The increased supply of oxygen will buoy you up and give you courage. The great tenor, Jean de Reszke, used to say that when you had your breath so you "could sit on it" nervousness vanished.

In every age, in every clime, men have always admired courage; so, no matter how your heart may be pounding inside, stride forth bravely, stop, stand still and act as if you loved it.

Draw yourself up to your full height, look your audience straight in the eyes, and begin to talk as confidently as if every one of them owed you money. Imagine that they do. Imagine that they have assembled there to beg you for an extension of credit. The psychological effect on you will be beneficial.

Do not nervously button and unbutton your coat, play with your beads, or fumble with your hands. If you must make nervous movements, place your hands behind your back and twist your fingers there where no one can see the performance—or wiggle your toes.

As a general rule, it is bad for a speaker to hide behind furniture; but it may give you a little courage the first few times to stand behind a table or chair and to grip them tightly—or hold a coin firmly in the palm of your hand.

How did Teddy Roosevelt develop his characteristic courage and self-reliance? Was he endowed by nature with a venturesome and daring spirit? Not at all. "Having been a rather sickly and awkward boy," he confesses in his *Autobiography*, "I was, as a young man, at first both nervous and distrustful of my own prowess. I had to train myself painfully and laboriously not merely as regards my body but as regards my soul and spirit."

Fortunately, he has told us how he achieved the transformation: "When a boy," he writes, "I read a passage in one of Marryat's books which always impressed me. In this passage the captain of some small British man-of-war is explaining to the hero how to acquire the quality of fearlessness. He says that at the outset almost every man is frightened when he goes into action, but that the course to follow is for the man to keep such a grip on himself that he can act just as if he were not frightened. After this is kept up long enough, it changes from pretense to reality, and the man does in very fact become fearless by sheer dint of practicing fearlessness when he does not feel it. (I am using my own language, not Marryat's.)

"This was the theory upon which I went. There were all kinds of things of which I was afraid at first, ranging from grizzly bears to 'mean' horses and gun-fighters; but by acting as if I was not afraid I gradually ceased to be afraid. Most men can have the same experience if they choose."

You can have that very experience, too, if you wish.

"In war," said Marshal Foch, "the best defensive is an offensive." So take the offensive against your fears. Go out to meet them, battle them, conquer them by sheer boldness at every opportunity.

Have a message, and then think of yourself as a Western Union boy instructed to deliver it. We pay slight attention to the boy. It is the telegram that we want. The message that is the thing. Keep your mind on it. Keep your heart in it. Know it like the back of your hand. Believe it feelingly.

Then talk as if you were determined to say it. Do that, and the chances are ten to one that you will soon be master of the occasion and master of yourself.

Fourth: Practice! practice! practice!

The last point we have to make here is emphatically the most important. Even though you forget everything you have read so far, do remember this: the first way, the last way, the never-failing way to develop self-confidence in speaking is—to speak. Really the whole matter finally simmers down to but one essential; practice, practice, practice. That is the sine qua non of it all, "the without which not."

"Any beginner," warned Roosevelt, "is apt to

have 'buck fever.' 'Buck fever' means a state of intense nervous excitement which may be entirely divorced from timidity. It may affect a man the first time he has to speak to a large audience just as it may affect him the first time he sees a buck or goes into battle. What such a man needs is not courage, but nerve control, coolheadedness. This he can get only by actual practice. He must, by custom and repeated exercise of self-mastery, get his nerves thoroughly under control. This is largely a matter of habit; in the sense of repeated effort and repeated exercise of will power. If the man has the right stuff in him, he will grow stronger and stronger with each exercise of it."

You want to get rid of your audience fear? Let us see what causes it.

"Fear is begotten of ignorance and uncertainty," says Professor Robinson in *The Mind in the Making*. To put it another way: it is the result of a lack of confidence.

And what causes that? It is the result of not knowing what you can really do. And not knowing what you can do is caused by a lack of experience. When you get a record of successful experience behind you, your fears will vanish; they will melt like night mists under the glare of a July sun.

One thing is certain: the accepted way to learn to swim is to plunge into the water. You have been reading this book long enough. Why not toss it aside now, and get busy with the real work in hand.

Choose your subject, preferably one on which you have some knowledge, and construct a three-minute talk. Practice the talk: by yourself a number of times. Then give it, if possible, to the group for whom it is intended, or before a group of friends, putting into the effort all your force and power.

~

How to Open a Talk

I once asked Dr. Lynn Harold Hough, formerly president of Northwestern University, what was the most important fact that his long experience as a speaker had taught him. After pondering for a minute, he replied, "To get an arresting opening, something that will seize the attention immediately." He planned in advance almost the precise words of both his opening and closing. John Bright did the same thing. Gladstone did it. Webster did it. Lincoln did it. Practically every speaker with common sense and experience does it.

But does the beginner? Seldom. Planning takes time, requires thought, demands will power. Cerebration is a painful process. Thomas Edison had this quotation from Sir Joshua Reynolds nailed on the walls of his plants: 'There is no expedient to which a man will not resort to avoid the real labor of thinking.' The tyro usually trusts to the inspiration of the moment with the consequence that he finds:

Beset with pitfall and with gin,
The road he is to wander in.

The late Lord Northcliffe, who fought his way up from a meager weekly salary to being the richest and most influential newspaper owner in the British Empire, said that these five words from Pascal had done more to help him succeed than anything else he had ever read: "To foresee is to rule."

That is also a most excellent motto to have on your desk when you are planning your talk. Foresee how you are going to begin when the mind is fresh to grasp every word you utter. Foresee what impression you are going to leave last—when nothing else follows to obliterate it.

Ever since the days of Aristotle, books on this subject have divided the speech into three sections: the introduction, the body, the conclusion. Until comparatively recently, the introduction often was, and could really afford to be, as leisurely as a buggy ride. The speaker then was both a bringer of news and an entertainer. A hundred years ago he often filled the niche in the community that is filled today by the newspaper, the magazine, the radio, television, the telephone, the movie theater.

But conditions have altered amazingly. The world has been made over. Inventions have speeded up life more in the last hundred years than they had formerly in all the ages since Belshazzar and Nebuchadnezzar. Automobiles, aeroplanes, radio, television; we are moving with increasing speed. And the speaker must fall in line with the impatient tempo of the times. If you are going to use an introduction, believe me, it ought to be short as a billboard advertisement.

This is about the temper of the average modern audience: "Got anything to say? All right, let's have it quickly and with very little trimmings. No oratory! Give us the facts quickly and sit down."

When Woodrow Wilson addressed Congress

on such a momentous question as an ultimatum on submarine warfare, he announced his topic and centered the audience's attention on the suhject with just twenty-three words: "A situation has arisen in the foreign relations of the country of which it is my plain duty to inform you very frankly."

The sales manager for the National Cash Register Company opened one of his talks to his men in this fashion. Only three sentences in this introduction; and they are all easy to listen to, they all have vigor and drive: 'You men who get the orders are the chaps who are supposed to keep the smoke coming out of the factory chimney. The volume of smoke emitted from our chimney during the past two summer months hasn't been large enough to darken the landscape to any great extent. Now that the dog days are over and the business revival season has begun, we are addressing to you a short, sharp request on this subject: We want more smoke.'

But do inexperienced speakers usually achieve such commendable swiftness and succinctness in their openings?

The majority of untrained and unskilled speakers will begin in one of two ways—both of which are bad. Let us discuss them forthwith.

Beware of opening with a so-called humorous story

For some lamentable reason, the novice often feels that he ought to be funny as a speaker. He may, by nature, mind you, be as solemn as the encyclopedia, utterly devoid of the lighter touch; yet the moment he stands up to talk he imagines he feels, or ought to feel, the spirit of Mark Twain descending upon him. So he is inclined to open with a humorous story, especially if the occasion is an after-dinner affair. What happens? The chances are twenty to one that the narration, the manner of this newly turned raconteur, is as heavy as the dictionary. The chances are his stories don't "click." In the immortal language of the immortal Hamlet, they prove "weary, stale, fiat and unprofitable."

If an entertainer were to misfire a few times like that before an audience that had paid for their seats, they would "boo" and shout "give him the hook." But the average group listening to a speaker is very sympathetic; so, out of sheer charity, they will do their best to manufacture a few chuckles; while, deep in their hearts, they pity the would-be humorous speaker for his failure! They themselves feel uncomfortable. Haven't you witnessed this kind of fiasco time after time?

In all the difficult realm of speech making, what is more difficult, more rare, than the ability to make an audience laugh? Humor is a hair-trigger affair; it is so much a matter of individuality, of personality.

Remember, it is seldom the story that is funny of, by, and in itself. It is the way it is told that makes it a success...

You may be one of those fortunately endowed individuals who has the rare gift of humor. If so, by all means, cultivate it. You will be thrice welcome wherever you speak. But if your talent lies in other directions, it is folly—and it ought to be high treason—for you to attempt to wear the mantle of Chauncey M. Depew.

Were you to study his speeches, and Lincoln's, and Job Hedges', you would probably be surprised at the few stories they told, especially in their openings. Edwin James Cattell confided to me that he had never told a funny story for the mere sake of humor. It had to be relevant, had to illustrate a point. Humor ought to be merely the frosting on the cake, merely the chocolate between the layers, not the cake itself. Strickland Gillilan, one of the best humorous lecturers in these United States, made it a rule never to tell a story during the first three minutes of his talk. If he found that practice advisable, I wonder if you and I would not also.

Must the opening, then, be heavy-footed, elephantine and excessively solemn? Not at all. Tickle our risibilities, if you can, by some local reference, something anent the occasion or the remarks of some other speaker. Observe some incongruity. Exaggerate it. That brand of humor is

forty times more likely to succeed than stale jokes about Pat and Mike, or a mother-in-law, or a goat.

Perhaps the easiest way to create merriment is to tell a joke on yourself. Depict yourself in some ridiculous and embarrassing situation. That gets down to the very essence of much humor…

Almost anyone can make an audience laugh by grouping incongruous ideas or qualities as, for example, the statement of a newspaper writer that he "hated children, tripe, and Democrats."

Note how cleverly Rudyard Kipling raised laughs in this opening to one of his political talks in England. He is retailing here, not manufactured anecdotes, but some of his own experiences and playfully stressing their incongruities:

> My Lords, Ladies and Gentlemen: When I was a young man in India I used to report criminal cases for the newspaper that employed me. It was interesting work because it introduced me to forgers and embezzlers and murderers and enterprising sportsmen of that kind. (Laughter.) Sometimes, after I had reported their trials, I used to visit my friends in jail when they were doing their sentences. (Laughter.) I remember one man who got off with a life sentence for murder. He was a clever, smooth-speaking chap, and he told me what he called the story of his life. He said: "Take it from me that when a man gets crooked, one thing leads to another until he finds himself in such a position that he has to put somebody out of the way to get straight again."
>
> (Laughter.) Well, that exactly describes the present position of the cabinet. (Laughter and cheers.)

This is the way William Howard Taft managed a bit of humor at the annual banquet of the superintendents of the Metropolitan Life Insurance Company. The beautiful part of it is this: he is humorous and pays his audience a gracious compliment at the same time:

> Mr. President and Gentlemen of the Metropolitan Life Insurance Company:
>
> I was out in my old home about nine months ago, and I heard an after-dinner speech there by a gentleman who had some trepidation in making it; and he said he had consulted a friend of his, who had had a great deal of experience in making after-dinner speeches, which friend advised him that the best kind of audience to address, as an after-dinner speaker, was an audience intelligent and well-educated but half-tight. (Laughter and applause.) Now, all I can say is that this audience is one of the best audiences I ever saw for an after-dinner speaker. Something has made up for the absence of that element that the remark implied (applause), and I must think it is the spirit of the Metropolitan Life Insurance Company. (Prolonged applause.)

Do not begin with an apology

The second egregious blunder that the beginner is wont to make in his opening, is this: He apologizes.

"I am no speaker I am not prepared to talk… I have nothing to say "Don't! Don't! The opening words of a poem by Kipling are: "There's no use in going further." That is precisely the way an audience feels when a speaker opens in that fashion.

Anyway, if you are not prepared, some of us will discover it without your assistance. Others will not. Why call their attention to it? Why insult your audience by suggesting that you did not think them worth preparing for, that just any old thing you happened to have on the fire would be good enough to serve them? No. No. We don't want to hear your apologies. We are there to be informed and interested, to be interested, remember that.

The moment you come before the audience, you have our attention naturally, inevitably. It is not difficult to get it for the next five seconds, but it is difficult to hold it for the next five minutes. If you once lose it, it will be doubly difficult to win it back. So begin with something interesting in your very first sentence. Not the second. Not the third. The first! F-I-R-S-T. First!

"How?" you ask. Rather a large order, I admit. And in attempting to harvest the material to fill it, we must tread our way down devious and dubious paths, for so much depends upon you, upon your audience, your subject, your material, the occasion, and so on…

Arouse curiosity

Here is an opening used by Mr. Howell Healy in a talk given at the Penn Athletic, Philadelphia. Do you like it? Does it get your interest immediately?

> Eighty-two years ago, and just about this time of year, there was published in London a little volume, a story, which was destined to become immortal. Many people have called it "the greatest little book in the world."
>
> When it first appeared, friends meeting one another on the Strand or Pall Mall, asked the question, "Have you read it?" The answer invariably was; "Yes, God bless him, I have."
>
> The day it was published a thousand copies were sold. Within a fortnight, the demand had consumed fifteen thousand. Since then it has run into countless editions, and has been translated into every language under heaven. A few years ago J. P. Morgan purchased the original manuscript for a fabulous sum; it now reposes among his other priceless treasures in

> that magnificent art gallery in New York City which he calls his library.
>
> What is this world-famous book? Dickens' *Christmas Carol*...

Do you consider that a successful opening? Did it hold your attention, heighten your interest as it progressed?

Why? Was it not because it aroused your curiosity, held you in suspense? Curiosity! Who is not susceptible to it?

The student who opened his talk with this question: Do you know that slavery exists in seventeen nations of the world today? not only aroused curiosity, but in addition, he shocked his auditors. "Slavery? Today? Seventeen countries? Seems incredible. What nations? Where are they?"

One can often arouse curiosity by beginning with an effect, and making people anxious to hear the cause.

An article in The Saturday Evening Post, entitled "With the Gangsters," began: "Are gangsters really organized? As a rule they are. How?" With ten words, you see, the writer of that article announced his subject, told you something about it, and aroused your curiosity as to how gangsters are organized. Very creditable. Every person who aspires to speak in public ought to study the technique that magazine writers employ to hook the reader's interest immediately. You can learn far more from them about how to open a speech than you can by studying collections of printed speeches.

Why not begin with a story?

We especially like to hear a speaker relate narratives from his own experience. Russell E. Conwell delivered his lecture, "Acres of Diamonds," over six thousand times, and received millions for it. And how does this marvelously popular lecture begin?

"In 1870 we went down the Tigris River. We hired a guide at Bagdad to show us Persepolis, Nineveh, and Babylon..."

And he is off—with a story. That is what hooks the attention. That kind of opening is almost foolproof. It can hardly fail. It moves. It marches. We follow. We want to know what is going to happen.

Here are opening sentences taken from two stories that appeared in a single issue of *The Saturday Evening Post*:

1. The sharp crack of a revolver punctuated the silence.
2. An incident, trivial in itself but not at all trivial in its possible consequences, occurred at the Montview Hotel, Denver, during the first week of July. It so aroused the curiosity of Goebel, the resident manager, that he referred it to Steve Faraday, owner of the Montview and half a dozen other Faraday hotels, when Steve made his regular visit a few days later on his midsummer swing of inspection.

Note that those openings have action. They start something. They arouse your curiosity. You want to read on; you want to know more; you want to find out what it is all about.

Even the unpracticed beginner can usually manage a successful opening if he employs the story technique and arouses our curiosity.

Begin with a specific illustration

It is difficult, it is arduous, for the average audience to follow abstract statements very long. Illustrations are easier to listen to, far easier. Then, why not start with one? It is hard to get speakers to do that. I know. I have tried. They feel somehow that they must first make a few general statements. Not at all. Open with your illustration, arouse the interest; then follow with your general remarks.

Use an exhibit

Perhaps the easiest way in the world to gain attention is to hold up something for people to look at. Even savages and half-wits, and babes in the cradle and monkeys in a store window and dogs on the street will give heed to that kind of stimulus. It can be used sometimes with effectiveness before the most dignified audience. For example, Mr. S.S. Ellis, of Philadelphia, opened one of his talks by holding a coin between his thumb and forefinger, and high above his shoulder.

Naturally everyone looked. Then he inquired: "Has anyone here ever found a coin like this on the sidewalk? It announces that the fortunate finder will be given a lot free in such and such a real estate development. He has but to call and present this coin...." Mr. Ellis then proceeded to condemn the misleading and unethical practices involved.

Ask a question

Mr. Ellis' opening has another commendable feature. It begins by asking a question, by getting the audience thinking with the speaker, cooperating with him. Note that *The Saturday Evening Post* article on gangsters opens with two questions in the first three sentences: "Are gangsters really organized? ... How?" The use of this question key is really one of the simplest, surest ways to unlock the minds of your audience and let yourself in. When other tools prove useless, you can always fall back on it.

Why not open with a question from some famous man?

The words of a prominent man always have attention power; so a suitable quotation is one of the very best ways of launching a harangue. Do you like the following opening of a discussion on Business Success?

"The world bestows its big prizes both in money and honors for but one thing," says Elbert

Hubbard. "And that is initiative. And what is initiative? I'll tell you: it is doing the right thing without being told."

As a starter, that has several commendable features. The initial sentence arouses curiosity; it carries us forward, we want to hear more. If the speaker pauses skillfully after the words, "Elbert Hubbard," it arouses suspense. "What does the world bestow its big prizes for?" we ask. Quick. Tell us. We may not agree with you, but give us your opinion anyway.... The second sentence leads us right into the heart of the subject. The third sentence, a question, invites the audience to get in on the discussion, to think, to do a little something. And how audiences like to do things. They love it! The fourth sentence defines initiative.... After this opening the speaker led off with a human interest story illustrating that quality.

Tie your topic up to the vital interests of your hearers

Begin on some note that goes straight to the personal interests of the audience. That is one of the best of all possible ways to start. It is sure to get attention. We are mightily interested in the things that touch us significantly, momentously.

That is only common sense, isn't it? Yet the use of it is very uncommon. For example, I heard a speaker begin a talk on the necessity of periodic health examinations. How did he open? By telling the history of the Life Extension Institute, how it was organized and the service it was rendering. Absurd! Our hearers have not the foggiest, not the remotest, interest in how some company somewhere was formed; but they are stupendously and eternally interested in themselves.

Why not recognize that fundamental fact? Why not show how that company is of vital concern to them? Why not begin something like this? "Do you know how long you are expected to live according to life insurance tables? Your expectancy of life, as insurance statisticians phrase it, is two-thirds of the time between your present age and eighty. For example, if you are thirty-five now, the difference between your present age and eighty is forty-five; you can expect to live two-third of that amount, or another thirty years. Is that enough? No, no, we are all passionately eager for more. Yet those tables are based upon millions of records. May you and I, then, hope to beat them? Yes, with proper precaution, we may; but the very first step is to have a thorough physical examination..."

Then, if we explain in detail why the periodic health examination is necessary, the hearer might be interested in some company formed to render that service. But to begin talking about the company in an impersonal way. It is disastrous! Deadly!

The attention power of shocking facts

"A good magazine article," said S. S. McClure, the founder of an important periodical, "is a series of shocks."

They jar us out of our daydreams; they seize, they demand attention. Here are some illustrations: Mr. N.D. Ballantine, of Baltimore, began his address on "The Marvels of Radio" with this statement: "Do you realize that the sound of a fly walking across a pane of glass in New York can be broadcast by radio and made to roar away off in Central Africa like the falls of Niagara?"

Mr. Harry G. Jones, president of Harry G. Jones Company, of New York City, began his talk on the Criminal Situation with these words: "The administration of our criminal law," declared William Howard Taft, then Chief Justice of the Supreme Court of the United States, "is a disgrace to civilization."

That has the double advantage of being not only a shocking opening, but the shocking statement is quoted from an authority on jurisprudence.

Mr. Paul Gibbons, former president of the Optimist Club of Philadelphia, opened an address on Crime with these arresting statements:

"The American people are the worst criminals in the world. Astounding as that assertion is, it is true. Cleveland, Ohio, has six times as many murders as all London. It has one hundred and seventy times as many robberies, according to its population, as has London. More people are robbed every year, or assaulted with intent to rob, in Cleveland than in all England, Scotland and Wales combined. More people are murdered every year in St. Louis than in all England and Wales. There are more murders in New York City than in all France or Germany or Italy or the British Isles. The sad truth of the matter is that the criminal is not punished. If you commit a murder, there is less than one chance in a hundred that you will ever be executed for it. You, as a peaceful citizen, are ten times as liable to die from cancer as you would be to be hanged if you shot a man."

That opening was successful, for Mr. Gibbons

put the requisite power and earnestness behind his words. They lived. They breathed. However, I have heard other students begin their talks on the crime situation with somewhat similar illustrations; yet their openings were mediocre.

Why? Words. Words. Words. Their technique of construction was flawless, but their spirit was nil. Their manner vitiated and emaciated all they said.

The value of the seemingly casual opening

How do you like the following opening, and why?

Mary E. Richmond is addressing the annual meeting of the New York League of Women Voters in the days before legislation against child marriages:

"Yesterday, as the train passed through a city not far from here, I was reminded of a marriage that took place there a few years ago. Because many other marriages in this state have been just as hasty and disastrous as this one, I am going to begin what I have to say to-day with some of the details of this individual instance.

"It was on December 12th that a high-school girl of fifteen in that city met for the first time a junior in a nearby college who had just attained his majority. On December 15th, only three days later, they procured a marriage license by swearing that the girl was eighteen and was therefore free from the necessity of procuring parental consent. Leaving the city clerk's office with their license, they applied at once to a priest (the girl was a Catholic), but very properly he refused to marry them. In some way, perhaps through this priest, the child's mother received news of the attempted marriage.

"Before she could find her daughter, however, a justice of the peace had united the pair. The bridegroom then took his bride to a hotel where they spent two days and two nights, at the end of which time he abandoned her and never lived with her again."

Personally, I like that opening very much. The very first sentence is good. It forecasts an interesting reminiscence. We want to hear the details. We settle down to listen to a human interest story. In addition to that, it seems very natural. It does not smack of the study, it is not formal, it does not smell of the lamp… "Yesterday, as the train passed through a city not far from here, I was reminded of a marriage that took place there a few years ago."

Sounds natural, spontaneous, human. Sounds

like one person relating an interesting story to another. An audience likes that. But it is very liable to shy at something too elaborate, something that reeks of preparation with malice aforethought. We want the art that conceals art.

How to Close a Talk

Would you like to know in what parts of your speech you are most likely to reveal inexperience or inexpertness, inaptitude or finesse? In the opening and the closing. There is an old saying in the theater, referring, of course, to actors, that goes like this: "By their entrances and their exits shall ye know them."

The beginning and the ending! They are the hardest things in almost any activity to manage adroitly. For example, at a social function, aren't the most trying feats the graceful entrance and the graceful leave-taking? In a business interview, aren't the most difficult tasks the winning approach and the successful close?

The close is really the most strategic point in a speech; what one says last, the final words left ringing in the ears when one ceases—these are likely to be remembered longest. Beginners, however, seldom appreciate the importance of this coign of vantage. Their endings often leave much to be desired.

What are their most common errors? Let us discuss a few and search for remedies. First, there is the man who finishes with "That is about all I have to say on the matter; so I guess I will stop."

That is not an ending. That is a mistake. It reeks of the amateur. It is almost unpardonable. If that is all you have to say, why not round off your talk, and promptly take your seat and stop without talking about stopping. Do that, and the inference that that is all you have to say may, with safety and good taste, be left to the discernment of the audience.

Then there is the speaker who says all he has to say, but he does not know how to stop. I believe it was Josh Billings who advised people to take the bull by the tail instead of the horns, since it would be easier to let go.

This speaker has the bull by the frontal extremities, and wants to part company with him, but try as hard as he will, he can't get near a friendly fence or tree. So he finally thrashes about in a circle, covering the same ground repeating himself, leaving a bad impression… .

The remedy? An ending has to be planned sometime, doesn't it? Is it the part of wisdom to try to do it after you are facing an audience, while you are under the strain and stress of talking, while your mind must be intent on what you are saying? Or does common sense suggest the advisability of doing it quietly, calmly, beforehand?

Even such accomplished speakers as Webster, Bright, Gladstone, with their admirable command of the English language, felt it necessary to write down and all but memorize the exact words of their closings.

The beginner, if he follows in their footsteps, will seldom have cause to regret it. He ought to know very definitely with what ideas he is going to close. He ought to rehearse the ending several times, using not necessarily the same phraseology during each repitition, but putting the thoughts definitely into words.

An extemporaneous talk, during the process of delivery, sometimes has to be altered very materially, has to be cut and slashed to meet unforeseen developments, to harmonize with the reactions of one's hearers; so it is really wise to have two or three closings planned. If one does not fit, another may.

Some speakers never get to the end at all. Along in the middle of their journey, they begin to sputter and misfire like an engine when the gasoline supply is about exhausted; after a few desperate lunges, they come to a complete standstill, a breakdown. They need, of course, better preparation, more practice—more gasoline in the tank.

Many novices stop too abruptly. Their method of closing lacks smoothness, lacks finish. Properly speaking, they have no close; they merely cease suddenly, jerkily. The effect is unpleasant, amateurish. It is as if a friend in a social conversation were to break off brusquely and dart out of the room without a graceful leave-taking.

No less a speaker than Lincoln made that mistake in the original draft of his First Inaugural. That speech was delivered at a tense time. The black storm clouds of dissension and hatred were already milling overhead. A few weeks later, the cyclone of blood and destruction burst upon the nation. Lincoln, addressing his closing words to the people of the South, had intended to end in this fashion:

> In your hands, my dissatisfied fellow-countrymen, and not in mine, is the momentous

> issue of the civil war. The government will not assail you. You can have no conflict without being yourselves the aggressors. You have no oath registered in heaven to destroy the government, while I have a most solemn one to preserve, protect and defend it. You can forbear the assault upon it. I cannot shrink from the defense of it. With you and not with me is the solemn question of "Shall it be peace or a sword?"

He submitted his speech to Secretary Seward. Seward quite appropriately pointed out that the ending was too blunt, too abrupt, too provocative. So Seward himself tried his hand at a closing; in fact, he wrote two. Lincoln accepted one of them and used it, with slight modifications, in place of the last three sentences of the close he had originally prepared. The result was that his First Inaugural Address now lost its provocative abruptness and rose to a climax of friendliness, of sheer beauty and poetical eloquence:

> I am loth to close. We are not enemies but friends. We must not be enemies. Though passion may have strained, it must not break

> our bonds of affection. The mystic chords of memory, stretching from every battlefield and patriot's grave to every living heart and hearthstone all over this broad land, will swell the chorus of the Union when again touched, as surely they will be, by the better angel of our nature.

How can a beginner develop the proper feeling for the close of an address? By mechanical rules?

No. Like culture, it is too delicate for that. It must be a matter of sensing, almost of intuition. Unless a speaker can feel when it is done harmoniously, adroitly, how can he himself hope to do it? However, this feeling can be cultivated; this experience can be developed somewhat, by studying the ways in which accomplished speakers have achieved it. Here is an illustration, the close of an address by the then Prince of Wales before the Empire Club of Toronto:

> I am afraid, gentlemen, that I have departed from my reserve, and talked about myself a good deal too much. But I wanted to tell you, as the largest audience that I have been privileged to address in Canada, what I feel about my position

> and the responsibility which it entails. I can only assure you that I shall always endeavor to live up to that great responsibility and to be worthy of your trust.

A blind man listening to that talk would feel that it was ended. It isn't left dangling in the air like a loose rope. It isn't left ragged and jagged. It is rounded off, it is finished.

The famous Dr. Harry Emerson Fosdick spoke in the Geneva Cathedral of St. Pierre the Sunday after the opening of the sixth assembly of the League of Nations. He chose for his text: "All they that take the sword shall perish with the sword." Note the beautiful and lofty and powerful way in which he brought his sermon to a close:

> We cannot reconcile Jesus Christ and war—that is the essence of the matter. That is the challenge which to-day should stir the conscience of Christendom. War is the most colossal and ruinous social sin that afflicts mankind; it is utterly and irremediably unchristian; in its total method and effect it means everything that Jesus did not mean and it means nothing that he did mean; it is a more blatant denial of every

Christian doctrine about God and man than all the theoretical atheists on earth ever could devise. It would be worth while, would it not, to see the Christian Church claim as her own this greatest moral issue of our time, to see her lift once more as in our fathers' days, a clear standard against the paganism of this present world and, refusing to hold her conscience at the beck and call of belligerent states, put the kingdom of God above nationalism and call the world to peace? That would not be the denial of patriotism but its apotheosis.

Here today, as an American, under this high and hospitable roof, I cannot speak for my government, but both as an American and as a Christian I do speak for millions of my fellow citizens in wishing your great work, in which we believe, for which we pray, our absence from which we painfully regret, the eminent success which it deserves. We work in many ways for the same end—a world organized for peace. Never was an end better worth working for. The alternative is the most appalling catastrophe mankind has ever faced. Like gravitation in the physical realm, the law of the Lord in the moral realm bends for no man and no nation:

> "All they that take the sword shall perish with the sword."

But this collection of speech endings would not be complete without the majestic tones, the organ-like melody of the close of Lincoln's Second Inaugural. The late Earl Curzon, of Keddleston, Chancellor of Oxford University, declared that this selection was "among the glories and treasures of mankind...the purest gold of human eloquence, nay, of eloquence almost divine":

> Fondly do we hope, fervently do we pray, that this mighty scourge of war may speedily pass away. Yet if God wills that it continue until all the wealth piled by the bondsman's two hundred and fifty years of unrequited toil shall be sunk, and until every drop of blood drawn with the lash shall be paid by another drawn with the sword, as was said three thousand years ago, so still it must be said that "the judgments of the Lord are true and righteous altogether." With malice toward none; with charity for all; with firmness in the right, as God gives us to see the right, let us strive on to finish the work we are in; to bind up the nation's wounds; to care for

> him who shall have borne the battle, and for his widow and his orphan—to do all which may achieve and cherish a just and lasting peace among ourselves, and with all nations.

You have just read what is, in my opinion, the most beautiful speech ending ever delivered by the lips of mortal man. Do you agree with my estimate? Where, in all the range of speech literature, will you find more humanity, more sheer loveliness, more sympathy?

"Noble as was the Gettysburg Address," says William E. Barton in Life of Abraham Lincoln, "this rises to a still higher level of nobility.... It is the greatest of the addresses of Abraham Lincoln and registers his intellectual and spiritual power at their highest altitude."

"This was like a sacred poem," wrote Carl Schurz. "No American President had ever spoken words like these to the American people. America had never had a president who had found such words in the depths of his heart."

But you are not going to deliver immortal pronouncements as President in Washington or as Prime Minister in Ottawa or Canberra. Your problem, perhaps, will be how to close a simple talk before a group of social workers.

How shall you set about it? Let us search a bit. Let us see if we cannot uncover some fertile suggestions.

Summarize your points

Even in a short talk of three to five minutes a speaker is very apt to cover so much ground that at the close the listeners are a little hazy about all his main points. However, few speakers realize that. They are misled into assuming that because these points are crystal clear in their own minds, they must be equally lucid to their hearers.

Not at all. The speaker has been pondering over his ideas for some time. But his points are all new to the audience; they are flung at the audience like a handful of shot. Some may stick, but the most are liable to roll off in confusion. The hearers are liable, like Iago, to "remember a mass of things but nothing distinctly."

Some anonymous Irish politician is reported to have given this recipe for making a speech: "First, tell them that you are going to tell them; then tell them; then tell them that you have told them." Not bad, you know. In fact, it is often highly advisable to "tell them that you have told them." Briefly, of course, speedily—a mere outline, a summary.

Here is a good example. The speaker was a traffic manager for one of Chicago's railways:

"In short, gentlemen, our own back dooryard experience with this block device, the experience in its use in the East, in the West, in the North—the sound operating principles underlying its operation, the actual demonstration in the money saved in one year in wreck prevention, move me most earnestly and unequivocally to recommend its immediate installation on our Southern branch."

You see what he has done! You can see it and feel it without having heard the rest of the talk. He has summed up in a few sentences, in sixty-two words, practically all the points he has made in the entire talk.

Don't you feel that a summary like that helps? If so, make that technique your own.

Appeal for action

The closing just quoted is an excellent illustration of the appeal-for-action ending. The speaker wanted something done: a block device installed on the

Southern branch of his road. He based his appeal for it on the money it would save, on the wrecks it would prevent. The speaker wanted action, and he got it. This was not a mere practice talk. It was delivered before the board of directors of a certain railway, and it secured the installation of the block device for which it asked.

A terse, sincere compliment

"The great state of Pennsylvania should lead the way in hastening the coming of the new day. Pennsylvania, the great producer of iron and steel, mother of the greatest railroad company in the world, third among our agricultural states—Pennsylvania is the keystone of our business arch. Never was the prospect before her greater, never was her opportunity for leadership more brilliant."

With these words, Charles Schwab closed his address before the Pennsylvania Society of New York. He left his hearers pleased, happy, optimistic. That is an admirable way to finish; but, in order to be effective, it must be sincere. No gross flattery. No extravagances. This kind of closing, if it does not ring true, will ring false, very false. And like a false coin, people will have none of it.

A humorous close

"Always leave them laughing," said George Cohan, "when you say good-by." If you have the ability to do it, and the material, fine! But how? That, as Hamlet said, is the question. Each man must do it in his own individual way.

One would hardly expect Lloyd George to leave a gathering of Methodists laughing when he was talking to them on the ultrasolemn subject of John Wesley's Tomb; but note how cleverly he managed it. Note, also, how smoothly and beautifully the talk is rounded off:

I am glad you have taken in hand the repair of his tomb. It should be honored. He was a man who had a special abhorrence of any absence of neatness or cleanliness. He it was, I think, who said, "Let no one ever see a ragged Methodist." It is due to him that you never can see one. (Laughter.) It is a double unkindness to leave his tomb ragged. You remember what he said to a Derbyshire girl who ran to the door as he was passing and cried, 'God bless you, Mr. Wesley.' 'Young woman,' he answered, 'your blessing would be of more value if your face and apron were cleaner.' (Laughter.) That was his feeling about untidiness. Do not leave his grave untidy. If he passed along, that would hurt him more than anything. Do look after that. It is a memorable and sacred shrine. It is your trust. (Cheers.)"

Closing with a poetical quotation

Of all methods of ending, none are more acceptable, when well done, than humor or poetry. In fact, if you can get the proper verse or poetry for your closing, it is almost ideal. It will give the desired flavor. It will give dignity. It will give individuality. It will give beauty.

Rotarian Sir Harry Lauder closed his address to the American Rotarian delegates at the Edinburgh convention in this fashion:

"And when you get back home, some of you send me a postcard. I will send you one if you do not send me one. You will easily know it is from me because there will be no stamp on it. (Laughter.) But I will have some writing on it, and the writing will be this:

'Seasons may come and seasons may go,
Everything withers in due course, you know,
But there is one thing still blooms as fresh as the dew,

That is the love and affection I still have for you."

That little verse fits Harry Lauder's personality, and no doubt it fitted the whole tenor of his talk. Therefore, it was excellent for him. Had some formal and restrained Rotarian used it at the end of a solemn talk, it might have been so out of key as to be almost ridiculous. The longer I teach public speaking, the more clearly I see, the more vividly I feel, that it is impossible to give general rules that will serve on all occasions. So much depends upon the subject, the time, the place, and the man. Everyone must, as Saint Paul said, "work out his own salvation."

I was a guest at a farewell dinner given in honor of the departure of a certain professional man from New York City. A dozen speakers stood up in tum, eulogizing their departing friend, wishing him success in his new field of activity. A dozen talks, and only one ended in an unforgettable manner. That was one that closed with a poetical quotation. The speaker, with emotion in his voice, turned directly to the departing guest, crying: "And now, good-by. Good luck. I wish you every good wish that you can wish yourself! I touch my heart as the Easterns do:

May the peace of Allah abide with you.
Wherever you come, wherever you go,
May the beautiful palms of Allah grow.
Through days of labor and nights of rest,
May the love of Allah make you blest.
I touch my heart as the Easterns do:
May the peace of Allah abide with you."

The climax

The climax is a popular way of ending. It is often difficult to manage and is not an ending for all speakers nor for all subjects. But, when well done, it is excellent. It works up to a crest, a peak, getting stronger sentence by sentence... Lincoln used the climax in preparing his notes for a lecture on Niagara Falls. Note how each comparison is stronger than the preceding, how he gets a cumulative effect by comparing its age to Columbus, Christ, Moses, Adam, and so on:

"It calls up the indefinite past. When Columbus first sought this continent—when Christ suffered on the cross—when Moses led Israel through the Red Sea—nay, even when Adam first came from the hands of his Maker; then, as now, Niagara was roaring here. The eyes of that species of extinct giants whose bones fill the mounds of America have gazed on Niagara, as ours do now. Contemporary with the first race of men, and older than the first man, Niagara is as strong and fresh today as ten thousand years ago. The Mammoth and Mastodon, so long dead that fragments of their monstrous bones alone testify that they ever lived, have gazed on Niagara—in that long, long time never still for a moment, never dried, never frozen, never slept, never rested."

Be brief! Be brief!

Hunt, search, experiment until you get a good ending and a good beginning. Then get them close together.

The speaker who does not cut his talk to fit in with the prevailing mood of this hurried, rapid age will be unwelcome and, sometimes, positively disliked.

No less a saint than Saul of Tarsus sinned in this respect. He preached until a chap in the audience, "a young man named Eutycbus," went to sleep and fell out of a window and all but broke his neck. Even then Saul may not have stopped talking. Who knows? I remember a speaker, a doctor, standing up one night at the University Club, Brooklyn. It had been a long banquet. Many speakers had already talked. It was two o'clock in the morning when his turn came. Had he been endowed with tact and fine feeling and discretion, he would have said half a dozen sentences and let us go home. But did he? No, not he. He launched into a forty-five minute tirade against vivisection. Long before he was half-way through, his audience were wishing that he, like Eutychus, would fall out of a window and break something, anything, to silence him.

Mr. Lorimer, when editor of *The Saturday Evening Post*, told me that he always stopped a series of articles in the *Post* when they were at the height of their popularity, and people were clamoring for more. Why stop then? Why then of all times?

"Because," said Mr. Lorimer, "the point of satiation is reached very soon after that peak of popularity."

The same wisdom will apply, and ought to be applied, to speaking. Stop while the audience is still eager to have you go on.

The greatest speech Christ ever delivered, the Sermon on the Mount, can be repeated in five minutes. Lincoln's Gettysburg address has only ten sentences. One can read the whole story of creation in Genesis in less time than it takes to peruse a murder story in the morning paper...

Be brief! Be brief!

PREVENT WORRY AND STRESS FOR LASTING SUCCESS

If you want to avoid worry, do what Sir William Osler did: Live in "day-tight compartments". Don't stew about the future. Just live each day until bedtime. And the next time Trouble—with a capital T—comes gunning for you and backs you up in a corner, try the magic formula of Willis H. Carrier. And always remind yourself of the exorbitant price you can pay for worry in terms of your health.

In the spring of 1871, a young man picked up a book and read twenty-one words that had a profound effect on his future. A medical student at the Montreal General Hospital, he was worried about passing the final examination, worried about what to do, where to go, how to build up a practice, how to make a living.

The twenty-one words that this young medical student read in 1871 helped him to become the most famous physician of his generation. He organised the world-famous Johns Hopkins School of Medicine. He became Regius Professor of Medicine at Oxford—the highest honour that can be bestowed upon any medical man in the British Empire. He was knighted by the King of England. When he died, two huge volumes containing 1,466 pages were required to tell the story of his life.

His name was Sir William Osler. Here are the twenty-one words that he read in the spring of 1871—twenty-one words from Thomas Carlyle that helped him lead a life free from worry: "Our main business is not to see what lies dimly at a distance, but to do what lies clearly at hand."

Forty-two years later, on a soft spring night when the tulips were blooming on the campus, this man, Sir William Osler, addressed the students of Yale University. He told those Yale students that a man like himself who had been a professor in four universities and had written a popular book was supposed to have "brains of a special quality." He declared that that was untrue. He said that his intimate friends knew that his brains were "of the most mediocre character."

What, then, was the secret of his success? He stated that it was owing to what he called living in "day-tight compartments." What did he mean by that? A few months before he spoke at Yale, Sir William Osler had crossed the Atlantic on a great ocean liner where the captain standing on the bridge, could press a button and—presto!—there was a clanging of machinery and various parts of the ship were immediately shut off from one another—shut off into watertight compartments. "Now each one of you," Dr. Osler said to those Yale students, "is a much more marvelous organisation than the great liner, and bound on a longer voyage. What I urge is that you so learn to control the machinery as to live with 'day-tight compartments' as the most certain way to ensure safety on the voyage. Get on the bridge, and see that at least the great bulkheads are in working order. Touch a button and hear, at every level of your life, the iron doors shutting out the Past—the dead yesterdays. Touch another and shut off, with a metal curtain, the Future—the unborn tomorrows. Then you are safe—safe for today! Shut off the past! Let the dead past bury its dead. Shut out the yesterdays which have lighted fools the way to dusty death. The load of tomorrow, added to that of yesterday, carried today, makes the strongest falter. Shut off the future as tightly as the past. The future is today.

There is no tomorrow. The day of man's salvation is now. Waste of energy, mental distress, nervous worries dog the steps of a man who is anxious about the future. Shut close, then the great fore and aft bulkheads, and prepare to cultivate the habit of life of 'day-tight compartments'."

Did Dr. Osler mean to say that we should not make any effort to prepare for tomorrow? No. Not at all. But he did go on in that address to say that the best possible way to prepare for tomorrow is to concentrate with all your intelligence, all your enthusiasm, on doing today's work superbly today. That is the only possible way you can prepare for the future.

~

Would you like a quick, sure-fire recipe for handling worry situations—a technique you can start using right away? Then let me tell you about the method worked out by Willis H. Carrier, the brilliant engineer who launched the air-conditioning industry...

"When I was a young man," Mr. Carrier said, "I worked for the Buffalo Forge Company in Buffalo, New York. I was handed the assignment of installing a gas-cleaning device in a plant of the Pittsburgh Plate Glass Company at Crystal City, Missouri—a plant costing millions of dollars. The purpose of this installation was to remove the impurities from the gas so it could be burned without injuring the engines. This method of cleaning gas was new. It had been tried only once before—and under different conditions. In my work at Crystal City, Missouri, unforeseen difficulties arose. It worked after a fashion—but not well enough to meet the guarantee we had made.

"I was stunned by my failure. It was almost as if someone had struck me a blow on the head. My stomach, my insides, began to twist and turn. For a while I was so worried I couldn't sleep.

"Finally, common sense reminded me that worry wasn't getting me anywhere; so I figured out a way to handle my problem without worrying. It worked superbly. I have been using this same anti-worry technique for more than thirty years. It is simple. Anyone can use it. It consists of three steps:

"*Step I.* I analysed the situation fearlessly and honestly and figured out what was the worst that could possibly happen as a result of this failure.

No one was going to jail me or shoot me. That was certain. True, there was a chance that I would lose my position; and there was also a chance that my employers would have to remove the machinery and lose the twenty thousand dollars we had invested.

"*Step II.* After figuring out what was the worst that could possibly happen, I reconciled myself to accepting it, if necessary. I said to myself: This failure will be a blow to my record, and it might possibly mean the loss of my job; but if it does, I can always get another position. Conditions could be much worse; and as far as my employers are concerned—well, they realise that we are experimenting with a new method of cleaning gas, and if this experience costs them twenty thousand dollars, they can stand it. They can charge it up to research, for it is an experiment.

"After discovering the worst that could possibly happen and reconciling myself to accepting it, if necessary, an extremely important thing happened: I immediately relaxed and felt a sense of peace that I hadn't experienced in days.

"*Step III.* From that time on, I calmly devoted my time and energy to trying to improve upon the worst which I had already accepted mentally.

"I now tried to figure out ways and means by which I might reduce the loss of twenty thousand dollars that we faced. I made several tests and finally figured out that if we spent another five thousand for additional equipment, our problem would be solved. We did this, and instead of the firm losing twenty thousand, we made fifteen thousand.

"I probably would never have been able to do this if I had kept on worrying, because one of the worst features about worrying is that it destroys our ability to concentrate. When we worry, our minds jump here and there and everywhere, and we lose all power of decision. However, when we force ourselves to face the worst and accept it mentally, we then eliminate all those vague imaginings and put ourselves in a position in which we are able to concentrate on our problem.

"This incident that I have related occurred many years ago. It worked so superbly that I have been using it ever since; and, as a result, my life has been almost completely free from worry."

Now, why is Willis H. Carrier's magic formula so valuable and so practical, psychologically speaking? Because it yanks us down out of the great grey clouds in which we fumble around when we are blinded by worry. It plants our feet good and solid on the earth. We know where we stand. And if we haven't solid ground under us, how in creation can we ever hope to think anything through?

~

Would you like to see how someone else adopted Willis H. Carrier's magic formula and applied it to his own problem? Well, here is one example, from a New York oil dealer who was a student in my classes.

"I was being blackmailed!" this student began. "I didn't believe it was possible—I didn't believe it could happen outside of the movies—but I was actually being blackmailed! What happened was this: the oil company of which I was the head had a number of delivery trucks and a number of drivers. At that time, OPA regulations were strictly in force, and we were rationed on the amount of oil we could deliver to any one of our customers. I didn't know it, but it seems that certain of our drivers had been delivering oil short to our regular customers, and then reselling the surplus to customers of their own.

"The first inkling I had of these illegitimate

transactions was when a man who claimed to be a government inspector came to see me one day and demanded hush money. He had got documentary proof of what our drivers had been doing, and he threatened to turn this proof over to the District Attorney's office if I didn't cough up.

"I knew, of course, that I had nothing to worry about—personally, at least. But I also knew that the law says a firm is responsible for the actions of its employees. What's more, I knew that if the case came to court, and it was aired in the newspapers, the bad publicity would ruin my business. And I was proud of my business—it had been founded by my father twenty-four years before.

"I was so worried I was sick! I didn't eat or sleep for three days and nights. I kept going around in crazy circles. Should I pay the money—five thousand dollars—or should I tell this man to go ahead and do his damnedest? Either way I tried to make up my mind, it ended in nightmare.

"Then, on Sunday night, I happened to pick up the booklet on *How to Stop Worrying* which I had been given in my Carnegie class in public speaking. I started to read it, and came across the story of Willis H. Carrier. 'Face the worst,' it said. So I asked myself: 'What is the worst that can happen if I refuse to pay up, and these blackmailers turn their records over to the District Attorney?'

"The answer to that was: The ruin of my business—that's the worst that can happen. I can't go to jail. All that can happen is that I shall be ruined by the publicity.

"I then said to myself: 'All right, the business is ruined. I accept that mentally. What happens next?'

"Well, with my business ruined, I would probably have to look for a job. That wasn't bad. I knew a lot about oil—there were several firms that might be glad to employ me. I began to feel better. The blue funk I had been in for three days and nights began to lift a little. My emotions calmed down. And to my astonishment, I was able to think.

"I was clear-headed enough now to face Step III—improve on the worst. As I thought of solutions, an entirely new angle presented itself to me. If I told my attorney the whole situation, he might find a way out which I hadn't thought of. I know it sounds stupid to say that this hadn't even occurred to me before—but of course I hadn't been thinking, I had only been worrying! I immediately made up my mind that I would see my attorney first thing in the morning—and then I went to bed and slept like a log!

"How did it end? Well, the next morning my lawyer told me to go and see the District Attorney and tell him the truth. I did precisely that. When I finished I was astonished to hear the D.A. say that this blackmail racket had been going on for months and that the man who claimed to be a 'government agent' was a crook wanted by the police. What a relief to hear all this after I had tormented myself for three days and nights wondering whether I should hand over five thousand dollars to this professional swindler!

"This experience taught me a lasting lesson. Now, whenever I face a pressing problem that threatens to worry me, I give it what I call 'the old Willis H. Carrier formula'."

~

The great Nobel-Prize winner in medicine, Dr. Alexis Carrel, said: "Business men who do not know how to fight worry die young." And so do housewives and horse doctors and bricklayers.

A few years ago, I spent my vacation motoring through Texas and New Mexico with Dr. O.F.

Gober—one of the medical executives of the Santa Fe railway. His exact title was chief physician of the Gulf, Colorado and Santa Fe Hospital Association. We got to talking about the effects of worry, and he said: "Seventy per cent of all patients who come to physicians could cure themselves if they only got rid of their fears and worries. Don't think for a moment that I mean that their ills are imaginary," he said. "Their ills are as real as a throbbing toothache and sometimes a hundred times more serious. I refer to such illnesses as nervous indigestion, some stomach ulcers, heart disturbances, insomnia, some headaches, and some types of paralysis.

"These illnesses are real. I know what I am talking about," said Dr. Gober, "for I myself suffered from a stomach ulcer for twelve years.

"Fear causes worry. Worry makes you tense and nervous and affects the nerves of your stomach and actually changes the gastric juices of your stomach from normal to abnormal and often leads to stomach ulcers."

Dr. Joseph F. Montague, author of the book *Nervous Stomach Trouble*, says much the same thing. He says: "You do not get stomach ulcers from what you eat. You get ulcers from what is eating you."

Dr. W.C. Alvarez, of the Mayo Clinic, said, "Ulcers frequently flare up or subside according to the hills and valleys of emotional stress."

That statement was backed up by a study of 15,000 patients treated for stomach disorders at the Mayo Clinic. Four out of five had no physical basis whatever for their stomach illnesses. Fear, worry, hate, supreme selfishness, and the inability to adjust themselves to the world of reality—these were largely the causes of their stomach illnesses and stomach ulcers. Stomach ulcers can kill you....

Can any man possibly be a success who is paying for business advancement with stomach ulcers and heart trouble? What shall it profit a man if he gains the whole world—and loses his health? Even if he owned the whole world, he could sleep in only one bed at a time and eat only three meals a day...

Do you love life? Do you want to live long and enjoy good health? Here is how you can do it. I am quoting Dr. Alexis Carrel again. He said: "Those who keep the peace of their inner selves in the midst of the tumult of the modern city are immune from nervous diseases."

Can you keep the peace of your inner self in the midst of the tumult of a modem city? If you are a normal person, the answer is "yes". "Emphatically yes." Most of us are stronger than we realise. We have inner resources that we have probably never tapped. As Thoreau said in his immortal book, Walden:

> I know of no more encouraging fact than the unquestionable ability of man to elevate his life by a conscious endeavour. If one advances confidently in the direction of his dreams, and endeavours to live the life he has imagined, he will meet with a success unexpected in common hours.

Surely, many of the readers of this book have as much will power and as many inner resources as Olga K. Jarvey has...

Here is Olga K. Jarvey's story as she wrote it for me: "Eight and a half years ago, I was condemned to die—a slow, agonising death—of cancer. The best medical brains of the country, the Mayo brothers, confirmed the sentence. I was at a dead-end street, the ultimate gaped at me! I was young. I did not want to die! In my desperation, I phoned my doctor at Kellogg and cried out to him the despair in my heart. Rather impatiently he upbraided me: 'What's the matter, Olga, haven't you any fight in you? Sure, you will die if you keep on crying. Yes, the worst has overtaken you. O.K.—face the facts! Quit worrying! And then do something about it!' Right then and there I took an oath, an oath so solemn that the nails sank deep into my flesh and cold chills ran down my spine: 'I am not going to worry! I am not going to cry! And if there is anything to mind over matter, I am going to win! I am going to LIVE!'

"The usual amount of X-ray in such advanced cases, where they cannot apply radium, is 10 1/2 minutes a day for 30 days. They gave me X-ray for 14 1/2 minutes a day for 49 days; and although my bones stuck out of my emaciated body like rocks on a barren hillside, and although my feet were like lead, I did not worry! Not once did I cry! I smiled! Yes, I actually forced myself to smile.

"I am not so foolish as to imagine that merely smiling can cure cancer. But I do believe that a cheerful mental attitude helps the body fight disease. At any rate, I experienced one of the miracle cures of cancer. I have never been healthier than in the last few years, thanks to those challenging, fighting words of Dr. McCaffery: 'Face the facts: Quite worrying; then do something about it!"

The Essential Techniques of Problem Analysis

We must equip ourselves to deal with different kinds of worries by learning the three basic steps of problem analysis. The three steps are: 1. Get the facts. 2. Analyse the facts. 3. Arrive at a decision—and then act on that decision. Obvious stuff? Yes, Aristotle taught it—and used it. And you and I must use it too if we are going to solve the problems that are harassing us and turning our days and nights into veritable hells.

Let me show you all this as it works out in practice. Since the Chinese say one picture is worth ten thousand words, suppose I show you a picture of how one man put exactly what we are talking about into concrete action.

Let's take the case of Galen Litchfield—a man I have known for several years; one of the most successful American business men in the Far East. Mr. Litchfield was in China in 1942, when the

Japanese invaded Shanghai. And here is his story as he told it to me while a guest in my home:

"Shortly after the Japs took Pearl Harbour," Galen Litchfield began, "they came swarming into Shanghai. I was the manager of the Asia Life Insurance Company in Shanghai. They sent us an 'army liquidator'—he was really an admiral—and gave me orders to assist this man in liquidating our assets. I didn't have any choice in the matter. I could co-operate—or else. And the 'or else' was certain death.

"I went through the motions of doing what I was told, because I had no alternative. But there was one block of securities, worth $750,000, which I left off the list I gave to the admiral. I left that block of securities off the list because they belonged to our Hong Kong organisation and had nothing to do with the Shanghai assets. All the same, I feared I might be in hot water if the Japs found out what I had done. And they soon found out.

"I wasn't in the office when the discovery was made, but my head accountant was there. He told me that the Jap admiral flew into a rage, and stamped and swore, and called me a thief and a traitor! I had defied the Japanese Army! I knew what that meant. I would be thrown into the Bridge house!

"The Bridge house! The torture chamber of the Japanese Gestapo! I had had personal friends who had killed themselves rather than be taken to that prison. I had had other friends who had died in that place after ten days of questioning and torture. Now I was slated for the Bridge house myself!

"What did I do? I heard the news on Sunday afternoon. I suppose I should have been terrified. And I would have been terrified if I hadn't had a definite technique for solving my problems. For years, whenever I was worried I had always gone to my typewriter and written down two questions—and the answers to these questions:

1. What am I worrying about?
2. What can I do about it?

"I used to try to answer those questions without writing them down. But I stopped that years ago. I found that writing down both the questions and the answers clarifies my thinking. So, that Sunday afternoon, I went directly to my room at the Shanghai Y.M.C.A. and got out my typewriter.

I wrote:

1. What am I worrying about?

I am afraid I will be thrown into the Bridge house tomorrow morning.

"Then I typed out the second question:

2. What can I do about it?

"I spent hours thinking out and writing down the four courses of action I could take—and what the probable consequence of each action would be.

1. I can try to explain to the Japanese admiral. But he "no speak English". If I try to explain to him through an interpreter, I may stir him up again. That might mean death, for he is cruel, would rather dump me in the Bridge house than bother talking about it.

2. I can try to escape. Impossible. They keep track of me all the time. I have to check in and out of my room at the Y.M.C.A. If I try to escape, I'll probably be captured and shot.

3. I can stay here in my room and not go near the office again. If I do, the Japanese admiral will be suspicion, will probably send soldiers to get me and throw me into the Bridgehouse without giving me a chance to say a word.

4. I can go down to the office as usual on

Monday morning. If I do, there is a chance that the Japanese admiral may be so busy that he will not think of what I did. Even if he does think of it, he may have cooled off and may not bother me. If this happens, I am all right. Even if he does bother me, I'll still have a chance to try to explain to him. So, going down to the office as usual on Monday morning, and acting as if nothing had gone wrong gives me two chances to escape the Bridgehouse.

"As soon as I thought it all out and decided to accept the fourth plan—to go down to the office as usual on Monday morning—I felt immensely relieved.

"When I entered the office the next morning, the Japanese admiral sat there with a cigarette dangling from his mouth. He glared at me as he always did; and said nothing. Six weeks later—thank God—he went back to Tokyo and my worries were ended.

"As I have already said, I probably saved my life by sitting down that Sunday afternoon and writing out all the various steps I could take and then writing down the probable consequences of each step and calmly coming to a decision. If I hadn't done that, I might have floundered and hesitated and done the wrong thing on the spur of the moment. If I hadn't thought out my problem and come to a decision, I would have been frantic with worry all Sunday afternoon. I wouldn't have slept that night. I would have gone down to the office Monday morning with a harassed and worried look; and that alone might have aroused the suspicion of the Japanese admiral and spurred him to act.

"Experience has proved to me, time after time, the enormous value of arriving at a decision. It is the failure to arrive at a fixed purpose, the inability to stop going round and round in maddening circles, that drives men to nervous breakdowns and living hells. I find that fifty per cent of my worries vanishes once I arrive at a clear, definite decision; and another forty per cent usually vanishes once I start to carry out that decision.

"So I banish about ninety per cent of my worries by taking these four steps:

1. Writing down precisely what I am worrying about.
2. Writing down what I can do about it.
3. Deciding what to do.
4. Starting immediately to carry out that decision."

Why is [Galen Litchfield's] method so superb? Because it is efficient, concrete, and goes directly to the heart of the problem. On top of all that, it is climaxed by the third and indispensable rule: Do something about it. Unless we carry out our action, all our fact-finding and analysis is whistling upwind—it's a sheer waste of energy.

Why don't you employ Galen Litchfield's technique to one of your worries right now?

Question No. 1: What am I worrying about?

Question No. 2: What can I do about it?

Question No. 3: Here is what I am going to do about it.

Question No. 4: When am I going to start doing it?

Solving Worry Problems at Work

Now I am going to show you how one business executive eliminated not fifty per cent of his worries, but seventy-five per cent of all the time he formerly spent in conferences, trying to solve business problems... This concerns a very real person—Leon Shimkin, a partner and general manager of one of the foremost publishing houses in the United States: Simon and Schuster.

Here is Leon Shimkin's experience in his own words:

"For fifteen years I spent almost half of every business day holding conferences, discussing problems. Should we do this or that—do nothing at all? We would get tense; twist in our chairs; walk the floor; argue and go around in circles. When night came, I would be utterly exhausted. I fully expected to go on doing this sort of thing for the rest of my life. I had been doing it for fifteen years, and it never occurred to me that there was a better way of doing it. If anyone had told me that I could eliminate three-fourths of all the time I spent in those worried conferences, and three-fourths of my nervous strain—I would have thought he was a wild-eyed, slap-happy, armchair optimist. Yet I devised a plan that did just that. I have been using this plan for eight years. It has performed wonders for my efficiency, my health, and my happiness.

"It sounds like magic—but like all magic tricks, it is extremely simple when you see how it is done.

"Here is the secret: First, I immediately stopped the procedure I had been using in my conferences for fifteen years—a procedure that began with my troubled associates reciting all the details of what had gone wrong, and ending up by asking: 'What shall we do?' Second, I made a new rule—a rule that everyone who wishes to present a problem to me must first prepare and submit a memorandum answering these four questions:

Question 1: What is the problem?

("In the old days we used to spend an hour or two in a worried conference without anyone's knowing specifically and concretely what the real problem was. We used to work ourselves into a lather discussing our troubles without ever troubling to write out specifically what our problem was.)

Question 2: What is the cause of the problem?

("As I look back over my career, I am appalled at the wasted hours I have spent in worried conferences without ever trying to find out clearly the conditions which lay at the root of the problem.)

Question 3: What are all possible solutions of the problem?

("In the old days, one man in the conference would suggest one solution. Someone else would argue with him. Tempers would flare. We would often get clear off the subject, and at the end of the conference no one would have written down all the various things we could do to attack the problem.)

Question 4: What solution do you suggest?

("I used to go into a conference with a man who had spent hours worrying about a situation and going around in circles without ever once thinking through all possible solutions and then writing down: 'This is the solution I recommend.')

"My associates rarely come to me now with their problems. Why? Because they have discovered that in order to answer these four questions they have to get all the facts and think their problems through. And after they have done that they find, in three-fourths of the cases, they don't have to consult me at all, because the proper solution has popped out like a piece of bread popping out from an electric toaster. Even in those cases where consultation is necessary, the discussion takes about one-third the time formerly required, because it proceeds along an orderly, logical path to a reasoned conclusion.

"Much less time is now consumed in the house

of Simon and Schuster in worrying and talking about what is wrong; and a lot more action is obtained toward making those things right."

~

Another instance:

My friend, Frank Bettger, one of the top insurance men in America, tells me he not only reduced his business worries, but nearly doubled his income, by a similar method.

"Years ago," says Frank Bettger, "when I first started to sell insurance, I was filled with a boundless enthusiasm and love for my work. Then something happened. I became so discouraged that I despised my work and thought of giving it up. I think I would have quit—if I hadn't got the idea, one Saturday morning, of sitting down and trying to get at the root of my worries.

"1. I asked myself first: 'Just what is the problem?' The problem was: that I was not getting high enough returns for the staggering amount of calls I was making. I seemed to do pretty well at selling a prospect, until the moment came for closing a sale. Then the customer would say: 'Well, I'll think it over, Mr. Bettger. Come and see me again.' It was the time I wasted on these follow-up calls that was causing my depression.

"2. I asked myself: 'What are the possible solutions?' But to get the answer to that one, I had to study the facts. I got out my record book for the last twelve months and studied the figures.

"I made an astounding discovery! Right there in black and white, I discovered that seventy per cent of my sales had been closed on the very first interview! Twenty-three per cent of my sales had been closed on the second interview! And only seven per cent of my sales had been closed on those third, fourth, fifth, etc., interviews, which were running me ragged and taking up my time. In other words, I was wasting fully one half of my working day on a part of my business which was responsible for only seven per cent of my sales!

"3. 'What is the answer?' The answer was obvious. I immediately cut out all visits beyond the second interview, and spent the extra time building up new prospects. The results were unbelievable. In a very short time, I had almost doubled the cash value of every visit I made from a call!"

Can you apply these questions to your business problems? To repeat my challenge—they can reduce your worries by fifty per cent. Here they are again:

1. What is the problem?
2. What is the cause of the problem?
3. What are all possible solutions to the problem?
4. What solution do you suggest?

PICK UP THESE EASY, EFFECTIVE HABITS TO BEAT STRESS AND FATIGUE

Relax! Relax! Relax! Learn to relax while you are doing your work! Easy? No. You will probably have to reverse the habits of a lifetime. But it is worth the effort, for it may revolutionise your life!

To prevent fatigue and worry, the first rule is: Rest often. Rest before you get tired. Why is that so important? Because fatigue accumulates with astonishing rapidity...

Your heart pumps enough blood through your body every day to fill a railway tank car. It exerts enough energy every twenty-four hours to shovel twenty tons of coal on to a platform three feet high. It does this incredible amount of work for fifty, seventy, or maybe ninety years. How can it stand it? Dr. Walter B. Cannon, of the Harvard Medical School, explains it. He says: "Most people have the idea that the heart is working all the time. As a matter of fact, there is a definite rest period after each contraction. When beating at a moderate rate of seventy pulses per minute, the heart is actually working only nine hours out of the twenty-four. In the aggregate its rest periods total a full fifteen hours per day."

During World War II, Winston Churchill, in his late sixties and early seventies, was able to work sixteen hours a day, year after year, directing the war efforts of the British Empire. A phenomenal record. His secret? He worked in bed each morning until eleven o'clock, reading papers, dictating orders, making telephone calls, and holding important conferences. After lunch he went to bed once more and slept for an hour. In the evening he went to bed once more and slept for two hours before having dinner at eight. He didn't cure fatigue. He didn't have to cure it. He prevented it. Because he rested frequently, he was able to work on, fresh and fit, until long past midnight.

The original John D. Rockefeller made two extraordinary records. He accumulated the greatest fortune the world had ever seen up to that time and he also lived to be ninety-eight. How did he do it? The chief reason, of course, was because he had inherited a tendency to live long. Another reason was his habit of taking a half-hour nap in his office every noon. He would lie down on his office couch-and not even the President of the United States could get John D. on the phone while he was having his snooze!

~

If you can't take a nap at noon, you can at least try to lie down for an hour before the evening meal. It is cheaper than a highball; and, over a long stretch, it is 5,467 times more effective. If you can sleep for an hour around five, six, or seven o'clock, you can add one hour a day to your waking life. Why? How? Because an hour's nap before the evening meal plus six hours' sleep at night—a total of seven hours—will do you more good than eight hours of unbroken sleep.

Let me repeat: Do what your heart does—rest before you get tired—and you will add one hour a day to your waking life.

~

Here is an astounding and significant fact: Mental work alone can't make you tired. Sounds absurd. But a few years ago, scientists tried to find out how long the human brain could labour without reaching "a diminished capacity for work", the scientific definition of fatigue. To the amazement of these scientists, they discovered that blood passing through the brain, when it is active, shows no fatigue at all! If you took blood from the veins of a day labourer while he was working, you would find it full of "fatigue toxins" and fatigue products. But if you took a drop of blood from the brain of an Albert Einstein, it would show no fatigue toxins whatever at the end of the day.

So far as the brain is concerned, it can work "as well and as swiftly at the end of eight or even twelve hours of effort as at the beginning." The brain is utterly tireless. So what makes you tired?

Psychiatrists declare that most of our fatigue derives from our mental and emotional attitudes. One of England's most distinguished psychiatrists, J.A. Hadfield, says in his book *The Psychology of Power*: "the greater part of the fatigue from which we suffer is of mental origin; in fact exhaustion of purely physical origin is rare."

One of America's most distinguished psychiatrists, Dr. A.A. Brill, goes even further. He declares: "One hundred per cent of the fatigue of the sedentary worker in good health is due to psychological factors, by which we mean emotional factors."

What kinds of emotional factors tire the sedentary (or sitting) worker? Joy? Contentment? No! Never! Boredom, resentment, a feeling of not being appreciated, a feeling of futility, hurry, anxiety, worry—those are the emotional factors that exhaust the sitting worker, make him susceptible to colds, reduce his output, and send him home with a nervous headache. Yes, we get tired because our emotions produce nervous tensions in the body.

The Metropolitan Life Insurance Company pointed that out in a leaflet on fatigue: "Hard work by itself," says this great life-insurance company, "seldom causes fatigue which cannot be cured by a good sleep or rest. Worry, tenseness, and emotional upsets are three of the biggest causes of fatigue. Often they are to blame when physical or mental work seems to be the cause. Remember that a tense muscle is a working muscle. Ease up! Save energy for important duties."

Stop now, right where you are, and give yourself a check-up. As you read these lines, are you scowling at the book? Do you feel a strain between the eyes?

Are you sitting relaxed in your chair? Or are you hunching up your shoulders? Are the muscles of your face tense? Unless your entire body is as limp and relaxed as an old rag doll, you are at this very moment producing nervous tensions and muscular tensions. You are producing nervous tensions and nervous fatigue!

Why do we produce these unnecessary tensions in doing mental work? Josselyn says: "I find that the chief obstacle is the almost universal belief that hard work requires a feeling of effort, else it is not well done." So we scowl when we concentrate. We hunch up our shoulders. We call on our muscles to make the motion of effort, which in no way assists our brain in its work.

Here is an astonishing and tragic truth: millions of people who wouldn't dream of wasting dollars go right on wasting and squandering their energy with the recklessness of seven drunken sailors in Singapore.

What is the answer to this nervous fatigue? Relax! Relax! Relax! Learn to relax while you are doing your work! Easy? No. You will probably have to reverse the habits of a lifetime. But it is worth the effort, for it may revolutionise your life!

William James said, in his essay "The Gospel of Relaxation": "The American over-tension and jerkiness and breathlessness and intensity and agony of expression are bad habits, nothing more or less." Tension is a habit. Relaxing is a habit. And bad habits can be broken, good habits formed.

How do you relax? Do you start with your mind, or do you start with your nerves? You don't start with either. You always begin to relax with your muscles!

Let's give it a try. To show how it is done, suppose we start with your eyes. Read this paragraph through, and when you've reached the end, lean back, close your eyes, and say to your eyes silently: "Let go. Let go. Stop straining, stop frowning. Let go. Let go." Repeat that over and over very slowly for a minute.

Didn't you notice that after a few seconds the muscles of the eyes began to obey? Didn't you feel as though some hand had wiped away the tension? Well, incredible as it seems, you have sampled in that one minute the whole key and secret to the art of relaxing. You can do the same thing with the jaw, with the muscles of the face, with the neck, with the shoulders, the whole of the body.

But the most important organ of all is the eye. Dr. Edmund Jacobson of the University of Chicago has gone so far as to say that if you can completely relax the muscles of the eyes, you can forget all your troubles! The reason the eyes are so important in relieving nervous tension is that they burn up one-fourth of all the nervous energies consumed by the body. That is also why so many people with perfectly sound vision suffer from "eyestrain". They are tensing the eyes.

Vicki Baum, the famous novelist, says that when she was a child, she met an old man who taught her one of the most important lessons she ever learned. She had fallen down and cut her knees and hurt her wrist. The old man picked her up; he had once been a circus clown; and, as he brushed her off, he said: "The reason you injured yourself was because you don't know how to relax. You have to pretend you are as limp as a sock, as an old crumpled sock. Come, I'll show you how to do it." That old man taught Vicki Baum and the other children how to fall, how to do flip-flops, and how to turn somersaults. And always he insisted: "Think of yourself as an old crumpled sock. Then you've got to relax!"

You can relax in odd moments, almost anywhere you are. Only don't make an effort to relax. Relaxation is the absence of all tension and effort. Think ease and relaxation. Begin by thinking relaxation of the muscles of your eyes and your face, saying over and over: "Let go…let go…let go and relax." Feel the energy flowing out of your facial muscles to the centre of your body. Think of yourself as free from tension as a baby.

That is what Galli-Curci, the great soprano, used to do. Helen Jepson told me that she used to see Galli-Curci before a performance, sitting in a chair with all her muscles relaxed and her lower jaw so limp it actually sagged. An excellent practice—it kept her from becoming too nervous before her stage entrance; it prevented fatigue.

Here are five suggestions that will help you learn to relax:

1. Read one of the best books ever written on this subject: *Release from Nervous Tension*, by Dr. David Harold Fink.
2. Relax in odd moments. Let your body go limp like an old sock. I keep an old, maroon-coloured sock on my desk as I work—I keep

it there as a reminder of how limp I ought to be. If you haven't got a sock, a cat will do. Did you ever pick up a kitten sleeping in the sunshine? If so, both ends sagged like a wet newspaper. Even the yogis in India say that if you want to master the art of relaxation, study the cat. I never saw a tired cat, a cat with a nervous breakdown, or a cat suffering from insomnia, worry, or stomach ulcers. You will probably avoid these disasters if you learn to relax as the cat does.

3. Work, as much as possible, in a comfortable position. Remember that tensions in the body produce aching shoulders and nervous fatigue.
4. Check yourself four or five times a day, and say to yourself: "Am I making my work harder than it actually is? Am I using muscles that have nothing to do with the work I am doing?" This will help you form the habit of relaxing, and as Dr. David Harold Fink says: "Among those who know psychology best, it is habits two to one."
5. Test yourself again at the end of the day, by asking yourself: "Just how tired am I? If I am tired, it is not because of the mental

> work I have done but because of the way I have done it." "I measure my accomplishments," says Daniel W. Josselyn, "not by how tired I am at the end of the day, but how tired I am not." He says: "When I feel particularly tired at the end of the day, or when irritability proves that my nerves are tired, I know beyond question that it has been an inefficient day both as to quantity and quality."

~

Adopt these Four Good Working Habits that will help prevent fatigue and worry:

Good working habit no. 1: Clear your desk of all papers except those relating to the immediate problem at hand

Roland L. Williams, President of Chicago and North-western Railway, says: "A person with his desk piled high with papers on various matters will find his work much easier and more accurate if he clears that desk of all but the immediate problem on hand. I call this good housekeeping, and it is the number-one step towards efficiency."

If you visit the Library of Congress in

Washington, D.C., you will find five words painted on the ceiling—five words written by the poet Pope: "Order is Heaven's first law."

Order ought to be the first law of business, too. But is it? No, the average business man's desk is cluttered up with papers that he hasn't looked at for weeks. In fact, the publisher of a New Orleans newspaper once told me that his secretary cleared up one of his desks and found a typewriter that had been missing for two years!

The mere sight of a desk littered with unanswered mail and reports and memos is enough to breed confusion, tension, and worries. It is much worse than that. The constant reminder of "a million things to do and no time to do them" can worry you not only into tension and fatigue, but it can also worry you into high blood pressure, heart trouble, and stomach ulcers.

Dr. John H. Stokes, professor, Graduate School of Medicine, University of Pennsylvania, read a paper before the National Convention of the American Medical Association—a paper entitled "Functional Neuroses as Complications of Organic Disease". In that paper, Dr. Stokes listed eleven conditions under the title: "What to Look for in the Patient's State of Mind". Here is the first item on that list: "The sense of must or obligation; the unending stretch of things ahead that simply have to be done."

But how can such an elementary procedure as clearing your desk and making decisions help you avoid this high pressure, this sense of must, this sense of an "unending stretch of things ahead that simply have to be done"? Dr. William L. Sadler, the famous psychiatrist, tells of a patient who, by using this simple device, avoided a nervous breakdown. The man was an executive in a big Chicago firm. When he came to Dr. Sadler's office, he was tense, nervous, worried. He knew he was heading for a tailspin, but he couldn't quit work. He had to have help.

"While this man was telling me his story," Dr. Sadler says, "my telephone rang. It was the hospital calling; and, instead of deferring the matter, I took time right then to come to a decision. I always settle questions, if possible, right on the spot. I had no sooner hung up than the phone rang again. Again an urgent matter, which I took time to discuss. The third interruption came when a colleague of mine came to my office for advice on a patient who was critically ill. When I had finished with him, I turned to my caller and began to apologise for keeping him waiting. But he had brightened up. He had a completely different look on his face."

"Don't apologise, doctor!" this man said to Sadler. "In the last ten minutes, I think I've got a hunch as to what is wrong with me. I'm going back to my offices and revise my working habits. But before I go, do you mind if I take a look in your desk?"

Dr. Sadler opened up the drawers of his desk. All empty—except for supplies. "Tell me," said the patient, "where do you keep your unfinished business?"

"Finished!" said Sadler.

"And where do you keep your unanswered mail?"

"Answered!" Sadler told him. "My rule is never to lay down a letter until I have answered it. I dictate the reply to my secretary at once."

Six weeks later, this same executive invited Dr. Sadler to come to his office. He was changed—and so was his desk. He opened the desk drawers to show there was no unfinished business inside of the desk. "Six weeks ago," this executive said, "I had three different desks in two different offices—and was snowed under by my work. I was never finished. After talking to you, I came back here and cleared out a wagon-load of reports and old papers. Now I work at one desk, settle things as they come up, and don't have a mountain of unfinished business nagging at me and making me tense and worried. But the most astonishing thing is I've recovered completely. There is nothing wrong any more with my health!"

Charles Evans Hughes, former Chief Justice of the United States Supreme Court, said: "Men do not die from overwork. They die from dissipation and worry." Yes, from dissipation of their energies-and worry because they never seem to get their work done.

Good working habit no. 2: Do things in the order of their importance

Henry L. Dougherty, founder of the nation-wide Cities Service Company, said that regardless of how much salary he paid, there were two abilities he found it almost impossible to find.

Those two priceless abilities are: first, the ability

to think. Second, the ability to do things in the order of their importance.

Charles Luckman, the lad who started from scratch and climbed in twelve years to president of the Pepsodent Company, got a salary of a hundred thousand dollars a year, and made a million dollars besides—that lad declares that he owes much of his success to developing the two abilities that Henry L. Dougherty said he found almost impossible to find. Charles Luckman said: "As far back as I can remember, I have got up at five o'clock in the morning because I can think better then than any other time—I can think better then and plan my day, plan to do things in the order of their importance."

Franklin Bettger, one of America's most successful insurance salesmen, doesn't wait until five o'clock in the morning to plan his day. He plans it the night before—sets a goal for himself—a goal to sell a certain amount of insurance that day. If he fails, that amount is added to the next day—and so on.

I know from long experience that one is not always able to do things in the order of their importance, but I also know that some kind of plan to do first things first is infinitely better than extemporising as you go along.

If George Bernard Shaw had not made it a rigid rule to do first things first, he would probably have failed as a writer and might have remained a bank cashier all his life. His plan called for writing five pages each day. That plan and his dogged determination to carry it through saved him. That plan inspired him to go right on writing five pages a day for nine heartbreaking years, even though he made a total of only thirty dollars in those nine years-about a penny a day.

Good working habit no. 3: When you face a problem, solve it then and there if you have the facts necessary to make a decision. Don't keep putting off decisions.

One of my former students, the late H.P. Howell, told me that when he was a member of the board of directors of U.S. Steel, the meetings of the board were often long-drawn-out affairs—many problems were discussed, few decisions were made. The result: each member of the board had to carry home bundles of reports to study.

Finally, Mr. Howell persuaded the board of

directors to take up one problem at a time and come to a decision. No procrastination—no putting off. The decision might be to ask for additional facts; it might be to do something or do nothing. But a decision was reached on each problem before passing on to the next. Mr. Howell told me that the results were striking and salutary: the docket was cleared. The calendar was clean. No longer was it necessary for each member to carry home a bundle of reports. No longer was there a worried sense of unresolved problems.

A good rule, not only for the board of directors of U.S. Steel, but for you and me.

Good working habit no. 4: Learn to organise, deputise, and supervise.

Many a businessman is driving himself to a premature grave because he has never learned to delegate responsibility to others, insists on doing everything himself. Result: details and confusion overwhelm him. He is driven by a sense of hurry, worry, anxiety, and tension. It is hard to learn to delegate responsibilities. I know. It was hard for me, awfully hard. I also know from experience the disasters that can be caused by delegating authority to the wrong people. But difficult as it is to delegate authority, the executive must do it if he is to avoid worry, tension, and fatigue.

~

One of the chief causes of fatigue is boredom...

We rarely get tired when we are doing something interesting and exciting. For example, I recently took a vacation in the Canadian Rockies up around Lake Louise. I spent several days trout fishing along Corral Creek, fighting my way through brush higher than my head, stumbling over logs, struggling through fallen timber—yet after eight hours of this, I was not exhausted. Why? Because I was excited, exhilarated. I had a sense of high achievement: six cutthroat trout. But suppose I had been bored by fishing, then how do you think I would have felt? I would have been worn out by such strenuous work at an altitude of seven thousand feet.

Even in such exhausting activities as mountain climbing, boredom may tire you far more than the strenuous work involved. For example, Mr. S.H. Kingman, president of the Farmers and Mechanics Savings Bank of Minneapolis, told me of an incident that is a perfect illustration of that statement. In July, 1943, the Canadian government asked the Canadian Alpine Club to furnish guides to train the members of the Prince of Wales Rangers in mountain climbing. Mr. Kingman was one of the guides chosen to train these soldiers. He told me how he and the other guides—men ranging from forty-two to fifty-nine years of age—took these young army men on long hikes across glaciers and snow fields and up a sheer cliff of forty feet, where they had to climb with ropes and tiny foot-holds and precarious hand-holds. They climbed Michael's Peak, the Vice-President Peak, and other unnamed peaks in the Little Yoho Valley in the Canadian Rockies. After fifteen hours of mountain climbing, these young men, who were in the pink of condition (they had just finished a six-week course in tough Commando training), were utterly exhausted.

Was their fatigue caused by using muscles that had not been hardened by Commando training? Any man who had ever been through Commando training would hoot at such a ridiculous question! No, they were utterly exhausted because they were bored by mountain climbing. They were so tarred, that many of them fell asleep without waiting to eat.

But the guides—men who were two and three times as old as the soldiers—were they tired? Yes, but not exhausted. The guides ate dinner and stayed up for hours, talking about the day's experiences. They were not exhausted because they were interested.

When Dr. Edward Thorndike of Columbia was conducting experiments in fatigue, he kept young men awake for almost a week by keeping them constantly interested. After much investigation, Dr. Thorndike is reported to have said: "Boredom is the only real cause of diminution of work."

If you are a mental worker, it is seldom the amount of work you do that makes you tired. You may be tired by the amount of work you do not do. For example, remember the day last week when you were constantly interrupted. No letters answered. Appointments broken. Trouble here and there. Everything went wrong that day. You accomplished nothing whatever, yet you went home exhausted—and with a splitting head.

The next day everything clicked at the office. You accomplished forty times more than you did the previous day. Yet you went home fresh as a snowy-white gardenia. You have had that experience. So have I.

The lesson to be learned? Just this: our fatigue is often caused not by work, but by worry, frustration, and resentment.

And so what? What can you do about it? Well, here is what one stenographer did about it—a stenographer working for an oil company in Tulsa, Oklahoma. For several days each month, she had one of the dullest jobs imaginable: filling out printed forms for oil leases, inserting figures and statistics. This task was so boring that she resolved, in self-defence, to make it interesting. How? She had a daily contest with herself She counted the number of forms she filled out each morning, and then tried to excel that record in the afternoon. She counted each day's total and tried to better it the next day. Result? She was soon able to fill out more of these dull printed forms than any other stenographer in her division. And what did all this get her? Praise? No. Thanks? No. Promotion? No. Increased pay? No. But it did help to prevent the fatigue that is spawned by boredom. It did give her a mental stimulant. Because she had done her best to make a dull job interesting, she had more energy, more zest, and got far more happiness out of her leisure hours. I happen to know this story is true, because I married that girl.

Here is the story of another stenographer who found it paid to act as if her work were interesting. She used to fight her work. But no more. Her name is Miss Vallie G. Golden… Here is her story, as she wrote it to me:

"There are four stenographers in my office and each of us is assigned to take letters from several men. Once in a while we get jammed up in these assignments; and one day, when an assistant department head insisted that I do a long letter over, I started to rebel. I tried to point out to him that the letter could be corrected without being retyped—and he retorted that if I didn't do it over, he would find someone else who would! I was absolutely fuming! But as I started to retype this letter, it suddenly occurred to me that there were a lot of other people who would jump at the chance to do the work I was doing. Also, that I was being paid a salary to do just that work. I began to feel better. I suddenly made up my mind to do my work as if I actually enjoyed it—even though I despised it. Then I made this important discovery: if I do my work as if I really enjoy it, then I do enjoy it to some extent I also found I can work faster when I enjoy my work. So there is seldom any need now for me to work overtime. This new attitude of mine gained me the reputation of being a good worker. And when one of the department superintendents needed a private secretary, he asked for me for the job—because, he said, I was willing to do extra work without being sulky! This matter of the power of a changed mental attitude," wrote Miss Golden, "has been a tremendously important discovery to me. It has worked wonders!"

Without perhaps being conscious of it. Miss Vallie Golden was using the famous "as if" philosophy. William James counseled us to act "as if" we were brave, and we would be brave; and to act "as if" we were happy, and we would be happy, and so on.

Act "as if" you were interested in your job, and that bit of acting will tend to make your interest real. It will also tend to decrease your fatigue, your tensions, and your worries.

Harlan A. Howard made a decision that completely altered his life. He resolved to make a dull job interesting—and he certainly had a dull one:

washing plates, scrubbing counters, and dishing out ice-cream in the high-school lunch-room while the other boys were playing ball or kidding the girls. Harlan Howard despised his job—but since he had to stick to it, he resolved to study ice-cream—how it was made, what ingredients were used, why some ice-creams were better than others. He studied the chemistry of ice-cream, and became a whiz in the high-school chemistry course. He was so interested now in food chemistry that he entered the Massachusetts State College and majored in the field of "food technology". When the New York Cocoa Exchange offered a hundred-dollar prize for the best paper on uses of cocoa and chocolate—a prize open to all college students—who do you suppose won it? That's right. Harlan Howard.

When he found it difficult to get a job, he opened a private laboratory in the basement of his home.... Shortly after that, a new law was passed. The bacteria in milk had to be counted. Harlan A. Howard was soon counting bacteria for the fourteen milk companies in Amherst—and he had to hire two assistants.

Where will he be twenty-five years from now? Well, the men who are now running the business of food chemistry will be retired then, or dead; and their places will be taken by young lads who are now radiating initiative and enthusiasm. Twenty-five years from now, Harlan A. Howard will probably be one of the leaders in his profession, while some of his class-mates to whom he used to sell ice-cream over the counter will be sour, unemployed, cursing the government, and complaining that they never had a chance. Harlan A. Howard might never have had a chance, either, if he hadn't resolved to make a dull job interesting.

There was another young man who was bored with his dull job of standing at a lathe, turning out bolts in a factory. His first name was Sam. Sam wanted to quit, but he was afraid he couldn't find another job. Since he had to do this dull work, Sam decided he would make it interesting. So he ran a race with the mechanic operating a machine beside him. One of them was to trim off the rough surfaces on his machine, and the other was to trim the bolts down to the proper diameter. They would switch machines occasionally and see who could turn out the most bolts. The foreman, impressed with Sam's speed and accuracy, soon gave him a better job.

That was the start of a whole series of promotions. Thirty years later, Sam—Samuel Vauclain—was president of the Baldwin Locomotive Works. But he might have remained a mechanic all his life if he had not resolved to make a dull job interesting.

H.V. Kaltenborn—the famous radio news analyst—once told me how he made a dull job interesting. When he was twenty-two years old, he worked his way across the Atlantic on a cattle boat, feeding and watering the steers. After making a bicycle tour of England, he arrived in Paris, hungry and broke. Pawning his camera for five dollars, he put an ad in the Paris edition of *The New York Herald* and got a job selling stereopticon machines. If you are forty years old, you may remember those old-fashioned stereoscopes that we used to hold up before our eyes to look at two pictures exactly alike. As we looked, a miracle happened. The two lenses in the stereoscope transformed the two pictures into a single scene with the effect of a third dimension. We saw distance. We got an astounding sense of perspective.

Well, as I was saying, Kaltenborn started out selling these machines from door to door in Paris—

and he couldn't speak French. But he earned five thousand dollars in commissions the first year, and made himself one of the highest-paid salesmen in France that year. H.V. Kaltenborn told me that this experience did as much to develop within him the qualities that make for success as did any single year of study at Harvard. Confidence? He told me himself that after that experience, he felt he could have sold The Congressional Record to French housewives.

That experience gave him an intimate understanding of French life that later proved invaluable in interpreting, on the radio, European events.

How did he manage to become an expert salesman when he couldn't speak French? Well, he had his employer write out his sales talk in perfect French, and he memorised it. He would ring a door-bell, a housewife would answer, and Kaltenborn would begin repeating his memorised sales talk with an accent so terrible it was funny. He would show the housewife his pictures, and when she asked a question, he would shrug his shoulders and say: "An American...an American." He would then take off his hat and point to a copy of the sales talk in perfect French that he had pasted in the top of his hat. The housewife would laugh, he would laugh—and show her more pictures. When H.V. Kaltenborn told me about this, he confessed that the job had been far from easy. He told me that there was only one quality that pulled him through: his determination to make the job interesting. Every morning before he started out, he looked into the mirror and gave himself a pep talk: "Kaltenborn, you have to do this if you want to eat. Since you have to do it—why not have a good time doing it? Why not imagine every time you ring a door-bell that you are an actor before the footlights and that there's an audience out there looking at you. After all, what you are doing is just as funny as something on the stage. So why not put a lot of zest and enthusiasm into it?"

Mr. Kaltenborn told me that these daily pep talks helped him transform a task that he had once hated and dreaded into an adventure that he liked and made highly profitable.

When I asked Mr. Kaltenborn if he had any advice to give to the young men of America who are eager to succeed, he said: "Yes, go to bat with yourself every morning. We talk a lot about the importance of physical exercise to wake us up out of the half-sleep in which so many of us walk around. But we need, even more, some spiritual and mental exercises every morning to stir us into action. Give yourself a pep talk every day."

Is giving yourself a pep talk every day silly, superficial, childish? No, on the contrary, it is the very essence of sound psychology. "Our life is what our thoughts make it." Those words are just as true today as they were eighteen centuries ago when Marcus Aurelius first wrote them in his book of Meditations: "Our life is what our thoughts make it."

By talking to yourself every hour of the day, you can direct yourself to think thoughts of courage and happiness, thoughts of power and peace. By talking to yourself about the things you have to be grateful for, you can fill your mind with thoughts that soar and sing.

By thinking the right thoughts, you can make any job less distasteful. Your boss wants you to be interested in your job so that he will make more money. But let's forget about what the boss wants. Think only of what getting interested in your job will do for you. Remind yourself that it may double the amount of happiness you get out of life, for you spend about one half of your waking hours at your work, and if you don't find happiness in your work, you may never find it anywhere. Keep reminding yourself that getting interested in your job will take your mind off your worries, and, in the long run, will probably bring promotion and increased pay. Even if it doesn't do that, it will reduce fatigue to a minimum and help you enjoy your hours of leisure.

CAREFULLY AND CONSTANTLY MONITOR YOUR FINANCES TO GROW YOUR WEALTH

Where your money is concerned, you're in business for yourself! And it is literally "your business" what you do with your money. But what are the principles of managing our money? How do we begin to make a budget and a plan? Learn and follow the eleven rules of personal finance.

Seventy per cent of all our worries, according to a survey made by the *Ladies' Home Journal*, are about money. George Gallup, of the Gallup Poll, says that his research indicates that most people believe that they would have no more financial worries if they could increase their income by only ten per cent. That is true in many cases, but in a surprisingly large number of cases it is not true. For example, while writing this chapter, I interviewed an expert on budgets: Mrs. Elsie Stapleton—a woman who spent years as financial adviser to the customers and employees of Wanamaker's Department Store in New York and of Gimbel's.

She has spent additional years as an individual consultant, trying to help people who were frantic with worry about money. She has helped people in all kinds of income brackets, all the way from a porter who earned less than a thousand dollars a year to an executive earning one hundred thousand dollars a year. And this is what she told me: "More money is not the answer to most people's financial worries. In fact, I have often seen it happen that an increase in income accomplished nothing but an increase in spending—and an increase in headaches. "What causes most people to worry," she said, "is not that they haven't enough money, but that they don't know how to spend the money they have!" [You snorted at that last sentence, didn't you? Well, before you snort again, please remember that Mrs. Stapleton did not say that was true of all people. She said: "most people". She didn't mean you. She meant your sisters and your cousins, whom you reckon by the dozens.]

A lot of readers are going to say: "I wish this guy Carnegie had my bills to meet, my obligations to keep up—on my weekly salary. If he did, I'll bet he would change his tune." Well, I have had my financial troubles: I have worked ten hours a day at hard physical labour in the cornfields and hay barns of Missouri—worked until my one supreme wish was to be free from the aching pains of utter physical exhaustion. I was paid for that grueling work not a dollar an hour, nor fifty cents, nor even ten cents. I was paid five cents an hour for a ten-hour day.

I know what it means to live for twenty years in houses without a bathroom or running water. I know what it means to sleep in bedrooms where the temperature is fifteen degrees below zero. I know what it means to walk miles to save a nickel car-fare and have holes in the bottom of my shoes and patches on the seat of my pants. I know what it means to order the cheapest dish on a restaurant menu, and to sleep with my trousers under the mattress because I couldn't afford to have them pressed by a tailor.

Yet, even during those times, I usually managed to save a few dimes and quarters out of my income because I was afraid not to. As a result of this experience, I realised that if you and I long to avoid debt and financial worries, then we have to do what a business firm does: we have to have a plan for spending our money and spend according to that plan. But most of us don't do that. For example, my good friend, Leon Shimkin, general manager of [Simon and Schuster], pointed out to me a curious blindness that many people have in regard to their money. He told me about a bookkeeper he knows, a man who is a wizard at figures when working for his firm—yet when it comes to handling his personal finances! Well, if this man gets paid on Friday noon, let us say, he will walk down the street, see an overcoat in a store window that strikes his fancy, and buy it—never giving a thought to the fact that rent, electric lights, and all kinds of "fixed" charges have to come out of that pay envelope sooner or later. No—he has the cash in his pocket, and that's all that counts. Yet this man knows that if the company he works for conducted its business in such a slap-happy manner, it would end up in bankruptcy.

Here's something to consider—where your money is concerned, you're in business for yourself! And it is literally "your business" what you do with your money.

But what are the principles of managing our money? How do we begin to make a budget and a plan? Here are eleven rules.

Rule No. 1: Get the facts down on paper

When Arnold Bennett started out in London fifty years ago to be a novelist, he was poor and hard-pressed. So he kept a record of what he did with every sixpence. Did he wonder where his money was going? No. He knew. He liked the idea so much that he continued to keep such a record even after he became rich, world-famous, and had a private yacht.

John D. Rockefeller, Sr., also kept a ledger. He knew to the penny just where he stood before he said his prayers at night and climbed into bed.

You and I, too, will have to get notebooks and start keeping records. For the rest of our lives? No, not necessarily. Experts on budgets recommend that we keep an accurate account of every nickel we spend for at least the first month—and, if possible, for three months. This is to give us an accurate record of where our money goes, so we can draw up a budget.

Oh, you know where your money goes? Well, maybe so; but if you do, you are one in a thousand! Mrs. Stapleton tells me it is a common occurrence for men and women to spend hours giving her facts and figures, so she can get them down on paper—

then, when they see the result on paper, they exclaim: "Is that the way my money goes?" They can hardly believe it. Are you like that? Could be.

Rule No. 2: Get a tailor-made budget that really fits your needs

Mrs. Stapleton tells me that two families may live side by side in identical houses, in the very same suburb, have the same number of children in the family, and receive the same income—yet their budgeting needs will be radically different. Why? Because people are different. She says a budget has to be a personal, custom-made job.

The idea of a budget is not to wring all the joy out of life. The idea is to give us a sense of material security—which in many cases means emotional security and freedom from worry. "People who live on budgets," Mrs. Stapleton told me, "are happier people."

But how do you go about it? First, as I said, you must list all expenses. Then get advice.

Rule No. 3: Learn how to spend wisely

By this I mean: learn how to get the best value for your money. All large corporations have professional buyers and purchasing agents who do nothing but get the very best buys for their firms. As steward and manager of your personal estate, why shouldn't you do likewise?

Rule No. 4: Don't increase your headaches with your income

Mrs. Stapleton told me that the budgets she dreads most to be called into consultation on are family incomes of five thousand dollars a year. I asked her why. "Because," she said, "five thousand a year seems to be a goal to most American families. They may go along sensibly and sanely for years—then, when their income rises to five thousand a year, they think they have 'arrived'. They start branching out. Buy a house in the suburbs, 'that doesn't cost any more than renting an apartment'. Buy a car, a lot of new furniture, and a lot of new clothes—and the first thing you know, they are running into the red. They are actually less happy than they were before—because they have bitten off too much with their increase in income."

That is only natural. We all want to get more out of life. But in the long run, which is going to bring us more happiness—forcing ourselves to live within a tight budget, or having dunning letters in the mail and creditors pounding on the front door?

Rule No. 5: Try to build credit, in the event you must borrow

If you are faced with an emergency and find you must borrow, life-insurance policies, Defence Bonds and Savings Certificates are literally money in your pocket. However, be sure your insurance policies have a savings aspect, if you want to borrow on them, for this means a cash value. Certain types of insurance, called "term insurance", are merely for your protection over a given period of time and do not build up reserves. These policies are obviously of no use to you for borrowing purposes. Therefore, the rule is: Ask questions! Before you sign for a policy, find out if it has a cash value in case you have to raise money.

Now, suppose you haven't insurance you can borrow on, and you haven't any bonds, but you do own a house, or a car, or some other kind of collateral. Where do you go to borrow? By all means, to a bank! Banks all over this land are subject to strict regulation; they have a reputation to maintain in the community; the rate of interest they can charge is fixed firmly by law; and they will deal with you fairly. Frequently, if you are in a financial jam, the bank will go so far as to discuss your problems with you, make a plan, and help you work your way out of your worry and indebtedness. I repeat, I repeat, if you have collateral, go to a bank!

However, suppose you are one of the thousands who don't have collateral, don't own any property, and have nothing to offer as guarantee except your wages or salary? Then, as you value your life, heed this word of warning! Do not—do not—apply to the first "loan company" whose alluring advertisements you see in the paper. These people, to read some of their ads, are as generous as Santa Claus. Don't you believe it! However, there are some companies that are ethical, honest, and strictly on the level. They are doing a service to those people who are faced with illness or emergency and have to raise money. They charge a higher rate of interest than the banks, but they have to do this, for they take greater risks and have greater expenses in collecting. But, before doing business with any loan company, go to your bank, talk to one of its officers, and ask him to recommend a loan company that he knows to be fair. Otherwise—otherwise—well, I don't want to give you nightmares, but here is what can happen:

At one time a newspaper in Minneapolis conducted an investigation into loan companies that were supposedly operating within the regulations laid down by the Russell Sage Foundation. I know a man who worked on that investigation—his name is Douglas Lurton, and he is now editor of *Your Life* magazine. Doug Lurton tells me that the abuses he saw among the poorer class of debtors would make your hair stand on end. Loans that had begun as a mere fifty dollars had soared and multiplied to three and four hundred dollars before they were paid. Wages were garnished; and, frequently, the man whose wages were attached was fired by his company. In numerous instances, when the man was unable to pay, the loan sharks simply sent an appraiser into his home to "evaluate" his furniture—and cleaned out the home! People were found who had been paying on small loans for four and five years and still owed money! Unusual cases? To quote Doug Lurton: "In our campaign, we so flooded the court with cases of this sort that the judges cried uncle, and the newspaper itself had to set up an arbitration bureau to take care of the hundreds of cases."

How is such a thing possible? Well, the answer, of course, is in all sorts of hidden charges and extra "legal fees". Here is a rule to remember in dealing with loan companies: if you are absolutely certain, beyond the shadow of a doubt, that you can pay the money off quickly, then your interest will be low, or reasonably low, and you will get off fairly. But if you have to renew, and keep on renewing, then your interest can mount into figures that would make Einstein dizzy. Doug Lurton tells me that in some cases these additional fees had swollen the original indebtedness to two thousand per cent, or about five hundred times as much as a bank would charge!

Rule No. 6: Protect yourself against illness, fire, and emergency expenses

Insurance is available, for relatively small sums, on all kinds of accidents, misfortunes, and conceivable emergencies. I am not suggesting that you cover yourself for everything from slipping in the bathtub to catching German measles—but I do suggest that you protect yourself against the major misfortunes that you know could cost you money and therefore do cost you worry. It's cheap at the price.

Rule No. 7: Do not have your life-insurance proceeds paid to your widow in cash

If you are carrying life insurance to provide for your family after you're gone, do not, I beg of you, have your insurance paid in one lump sum.

What happens to "a new widow with new money"? I'll let Mrs. Marion S. Eberly answer that question. She is head of the Women's Division of the Institute of Life Insurance, 60 East 42nd Street, New York City. She speaks before women's clubs all over America on the wisdom of using life-insurance proceeds to purchase a life income for the widow instead of giving her the proceeds in cash. She tells me one widow who received twenty thousand dollars in cash and lent it to her son to start in the auto-accessory business. The business failed, and she is destitute now. She tells of another widow who was persuaded by a slick real-estate salesman to put most of her life-insurance money in vacant lots that were "sure to double in value within a year". Three years later, she sold the lots for one-tenth of what she paid for them. She tells of another widow who had to apply to the Child Welfare Association for the support of her children-within twelve months after she had been left fifteenth thousand dollars in life insurance. A hundred thousand similar tragedies could be told.

"The average lifetime of twenty-five thousand dollars left in the hands of a woman is less than seven years." That statement was made by Sylvia S. Porter, financial editor of the *New York Post*, in the *Ladies' Home Journal*.

Years ago, *The Saturday Evening Post* said in an editorial: "The ease with which the average widow without business training, and with no banker to advise her, can be wheedled into putting her husband's life-insurance money into wildcat stocks by the first slick salesman who approaches her- is proverbial. Any lawyer or banker can cite a dozen cases in which the entire savings of a thrifty man's lifetime, amassed by years of sacrifice and self-denial, were swept away simply because a widow or an orphan trusted one of the slick crooks who rob women for a livelihood."

If you want to protect your widow and your children, why not take a tip from J.P. Morgan— one of the wisest financiers who ever lived. He left money in his will to sixteen principal legatees. Twelve were women. Did he leave these women cash? No. He left trust funds that ensured these women a monthly income for life.

Rule No. 8: Teach your children a responsible attitude toward money

I shall never forget an idea I once read in *Your Life* magazine. The author, Stella Weston Turtle, described how she was teaching her little girl a sense of responsibility about money. She got an extra cheque-book from the bank and gave it to her nine-year-old daughter. When the daughter was given her weekly allowance, she "deposited" the money with her mother, who served as a bank for the child's funds. Then, throughout the week, whenever she wanted a cent or two, she "drew a cheque" for that amount and kept track of her balance. The little girl not only found that fun, but began to learn real responsibility in handling her money.

This is an excellent method and if you have a son or daughter of school age, and you want this child to learn how to handle money, I recommend it for your consideration.

Rule No. 9: If necessary, make a little extra money off your kitchen stove

If after you budget your expenses wisely you still find that you don't have enough to make ends meet, you can then do one of two things: you can either scold, fret, worry, and complain, or you can plan to make a little additional money on the side. How? Well, all you have to do to make money is to fill an urgent need that isn't being adequately filled now. That is what Mrs. Nellie Speer of ... Jackson Heights, New York, did. In 1932, she found herself living alone in a three-room apartment. Her husband had died, and both of her children were married. One day, while having some ice-cream at a drug-store soda fountain, she noticed that the fountain was also selling bakery pies that looked sad and dreary. She asked the proprietor if he would buy some real home-made pies from her. He ordered two. "Although I was a good cook," Mrs. Speer said, as she told me the story, "I had always had servants when we lived in Georgia, and I had never baked more than a dozen pies in my life. After getting that order for two pies, I asked a neighbor woman how to cook an apple-pie. The soda-fountain customers were delighted with my first two home-baked pies, one apple, one lemon. The drugstore ordered five the next day. Then orders gradually came in from other fountains and luncheonettes. Within two years, I was baking five thousand pies a year—I was doing all the work myself in my own tiny kitchen, and I was making a thousand dollars a year clear, without a penny's expense except the ingredients that went into the pies."

The demand for Mrs. Speer's home-baked pastry became so great that she had to move out of her kitchen into a shop and hire two girls to bake for her: pies, cakes, bread, and rolls. During the war, people stood in line for an hour at a time to buy her home-baked foods.

"I have never been happier in my life," Mrs. Speer said. "I work in the shop twelve to fourteen hours a day, but I don't get tired because it isn't work to me. It is an adventure in living. I am doing my part to make people a little happier. I am too busy to be lonesome or worried. My work has filled a gap in my life left vacant by the passing of my mother and husband and my home."

When I asked Mrs. Speer if she felt that other women who were good cooks could make money in their spare time in a similar way, in towns of ten thousand and up, she replied: "Yes—of course they can!"

Mrs. Ora Snyder will tell you the same thing. She lives in a town of thirty thousand—Maywood, Illinois. Yet she started in business with the kitchen stove and ten cents' worth of ingredients. Her husband fell ill. She had to earn money. But how? No experience. No skill. No capital. Just a housewife. She took the white of an egg and sugar and made some candy on the back of the kitchen stove; then she took her pan of candy and stood near the school and sold it to the children for a penny a piece as they went home. "Bring more pennies tomorrow," she said. "I'll be here every day with my home-made candy." During the first week, she not only made a profit, but had also put a new zest into living. She was making both herself and the children happy. No time now for worry.

This quiet little housewife from Maywood, Illinois, was so ambitious that she decided to branch out—to have an agent sell her kitchen-made candy in roaring, thundering Chicago. She timidly approached an Italian selling peanuts on the street. He shrugged his shoulders. His customers wanted peanuts, not candy. She gave him a sample. He liked it, began selling her candy, and made a good profit for Mrs. Snyder on the first day. Four years later, she opened her first store in Chicago. It was only eight feet wide. She made her candy at night and sold it in the daytime. This erstwhile timid housewife, who started her candy factory on her kitchen stove, now has seventeen stores—fifteen of them in the busy Loop district of Chicago.

Here is the point I am trying to make. Nellie Speer, in Jackson Heights, New York, and Mrs. Ora Snyder, in Maywood, Illinois, instead of worrying about finances, did something positive. They started in an extremely small way to make money off the kitchen stove—no overhead, no rent, no advertising, no salaries. Under these conditions, it is almost impossible for a woman to be defeated by financial worries.

Look around you. You will find many needs that are not filled. For example, if you train yourself to be a good cook, you can probably make money by starting cooking classes for young girls right in your own kitchen. You can get your students by ringing door-bells.

Books have been written about how to make

money in your spare time; inquire at your public library. There are many opportunities for both men and women. But one word of warning: unless you have a natural gift for selling, don't attempt door-to-door selling. Most people hate it and fail at it.

Rule No. 10: Don't gamble—ever

I am always astounded by the people who hope to make money by betting on the ponies or playing slot machines. I know a man who makes his living by owning a string of these "one armed bandits", and he has nothing but contempt for the foolish people who are so naive as to imagine that they can beat a machine that is already rigged against them.

I also know one of the best known bookmakers in America. He was a student in my adult-education classes. He told me that with all his knowledge of horse racing, he couldn't make money betting on the ponies. Yet the facts are that foolish people bet six billion dollars a year on the races—six times as much as our total national debt back in 1910. This bookmaker also told me that if he had an enemy he despised, he could think of no better way of ruining him than by getting him to bet on the races. When I asked him what would happen to the man who played the races according to the tipster sheets, he replied: "You could lose the Mint by betting that way."

If we are determined to gamble, let's at least be smart. Let's find out what the odds are against us. How? By reading a book entitled *How to Figure the Odds*, by Oswald Jacoby—an authority on bridge and poker, a top-ranking mathematician, a professional statistician, and an insurance actuary. This book devotes 215 pages to telling you what the odds are against your winning when you play the ponies, roulette, craps, slot machines, draw poker, stud poker, contract bridge, auction pinochle, the stock market. This book also give you the scientific, mathematical chances on a score of other activities. It doesn't pretend to show how to make money gambling. The author has no axe to grind. He merely shows you what the odds are against your winning in all the usual ways of gambling; and when you see the odds, you will pity the poor suckers who stake their hard-earned wages on horse races or cards or dice or slot machines. If you are tempted to shoot craps or play poker or bet on horses, this book may save you a hundred times—yes, maybe a thousand times—what it costs.

Rule No. 11: If we can't possibly improve our financial situation, let's be good to ourselves and stop resenting what can't be changed

If we can't possibly improve our financial situation, maybe we can improve our mental attitude towards it. Let's remember that other people have their financial worries, too. We may be worried because we can't keep up with the Joneses; but the Joneses are probably worried because they can't keep up with the Ritzes; and the Ritzes are worried because they can't keep up with the Vanderbilts.

Some of the most famous men in American history have had their financial troubles. Both Lincoln and Washington had to borrow money to make the trip to be inaugurated as President.

If we can't have all we want, let's not poison our days and sour our dispositions with worry and resentment. Let's be good to ourselves. Let's try to be philosophical about it.

"If you have what seems to you insufficient," said one of Rome's greatest philosophers, Seneca, "then you will be miserable even if you possess the world."

WORDS OF WISDOM TO INSPIRE YOU

Every new life is a new thing under the sun; there has never been anything just like it before, never will be again. A young man ought to get that idea about himself; he should look for the single spark of individuality that makes him different from other folks, and develop that for all he is worth. Society and schools may try to iron it out of him; their tendency is to put it all in the same mold, but I say don't let that spark be lost; it is your only real claim to importance.

—Henry Ford

Know what work you want to do and go after it. The young man who gets ahead must decide for what wishes to do. From his own tastes, his own enthusiasm, he must get the motive and the inspiration which are to start him on his way to a successful life.

—Alexander Graham Bell

~

People are always blaming their circumstances for what they are. I don't believe in circumstances. The people who get on in this world are the people who get up and look for the circumstances they want, and, if they can't find them, make them.

—George Bernard Shaw

A man can succeed at almost anything for
which he has unlimited enthusiasm.

—Charles Schwab

~

The longer I live, the more certain I am that enthusiasm is the little recognized secret of success. The difference in actual skill and ability and intelligence between those who succeed and those who fail is usually neither wide nor striking. But if two people are nearly equally matched, the one who is enthusiastic will find the scales tipped in his or her favor. And someone of second-rate ability with enthusiasm will often outstrip one of first-rate ability without enthusiasm.

—Frederick Williamson

If you want to win friends, make it a point to remember them. If you remember my name, you pay me a compliment; you indicate that I have made an impression on you. Remember my name and you add to my feeling of importance.

—Dale Carnegie

~

One of the surest ways of making a friend and influencing the opinion of another is to give consideration to his opinion, to let him sustain his feeling of importance.

—Dale Carnegie

One of the hardest things in this world to do is to admit you are wrong. And nothing is more helpful in resolving a situation than its frank admission.

—Benjamin Disraeli

~

If you can hold up your head and admit that you were in the wrong, then a wrong deed can benefit you. For to admit a wrong will not only increase the respect of those about you, it will increase your own self-respect.

—Dale Carnegie

Work is the true elixir of life. The busiest man is the happiest man. Excellence in any art or profession is attained only by hard and persistent work. Never believe that you are perfect. When a man imagines, even after years of striving, that he has attained perfection, his decline begins.

—Sir Theodore Martin

~

Tomorrow's fate, though thou be wise,
Thou canst not tell nor yet surmise;
Pass, therefore, not today in vain,
For it will never come again.

—Omar Khayyam

Give your problem all the thought you
possibly can before a solution is reached.
But when the matter is settled and over
with, worry not at all.

—Dale Carnegie

~

Our main business is not to see what lies
dimly at a distance, but to do
what lies clearly at hand.

—Thomas Carlyle

One may walk over the highest mountain—one step at a time.

—John Wanamaker

~

If time be of all things most precious, wasting time must be the greatest prodigality, since lost time is never found again; and what we call time enough always proves little enough. Let us then be up and doing, and doing to a purpose; so by diligence shall we do more with less perplexity.

—Benjamin Franklin

I know that I am considered an inveterate optimist and properly so. Why? Because I always turn my eyes toward success, not failure. I involuntarily turn my back on disaster and eliminate the hypothesis of failure. This is my philosophy in action. Every time you have a task before you, examine it carefully, take exact measure of what is expected of you. Then make your plan and, in order to execute it properly, create for yourself a method, never improvise.

—Marshal Ferdinand Foch

~

When I can't handle events,
I let them handle themselves.

—Henry Ford

Face your deficiencies and acknowledge them; but do not let them master you. Let them teach you patience, sweetness, insight. True education combines intellect, beauty, goodness, and the greatest of these is goodness. When we do the best we can, we never know what miracle is wrought in our life, or in the life of another.

—Helen Keller

~

If we did all the things we are capable of doing, we would literally astound ourselves.

—Thomas A. Edison

Perseverance is a great element of success. If you only knock long enough and loud enough at the gate, you are sure to wake up somebody.

—Henry W. Longfellow

~

Do a little more each day than you think you possibly can.

—Lowell Thomas

The person who accepts responsibility makes himself stand out from the others in an office, a factory or in any walk in life, and he is the one who gets ahead. Welcome responsibility. Do this in little things and in big things, and success will come to you.

—Dale Carnegie

~

Do the hard jobs first. The easy jobs will take care of themselves.

—Dale Carnegie

Finish each day and be done with it...
You have done what you could; some
blunders and absurdities no doubt
crept in; forget them as soon as you can.
Tomorrow is a new day; you shall
begin it well and serenely.

—Ralph Waldo Emerson

~

Today is a new day. You will get out
of it just what you put into it...If you
have made mistakes, even serious mistakes,
there is always another chance for you.
And supposing you have tried and failed
again and again, you may have a fresh
start any moment you choose, for this
thing that we call failure is not the falling
down, but the staying down.

—Mary Pickford

Face the thing that seems overwhelming
and you will be surprised how
your fear will melt away.

—Dale Carnegie

~

When you get into a tight place and
everything goes against you, till it seems
as though you could not hold on a minute
longer, never give up then, for that is just
the place and time that the tide will turn.

—Harriet Beecher Stowe

For all your days prepare,
And meet them ever alike:
When you are the anvil, bear—
When you are the hammer, strike.

—Edwin Markham

~

To improve the golden moment of opportunity, and catch the good that is within our reach, is the great art of life.

—Charles Kingsley

Don't let anything discourage you. Keep on. Never give up. That has been the policy of most of those who have succeeded. Of course discouragement will come. The important thing is to surmount it. If you can do that, the world is yours!

—Dale Carnegie

Lightning Source UK Ltd.
Milton Keynes UK
UKHW010718061118
331851UK00013B/1206/P

9 789388 070744